PrayerFoundation Evangelical Lay Monks ™
Answers to Prayer
A Global 24-Hr. Prayerchain Since 2000

by S.G. Preston

I0161315

*"I live in the spirit of prayer.
I pray as I walk about,
when I lie down, and when I rise up.
And the answers are always coming."*

-George Müller (1805-1898)

———

*"As white snowflakes fall quietly
and thickly on a winter day,
answers to prayer
will settle down upon you
at every step you take,
even to your dying day.*

*The story of your life
will be the story of prayer,
and answers to prayer."*

-O. Hallesby (1879-1961)

2nd Edition

PrayerFoundation Press ™
Vancouver, WA 98687 U.S.A.

There are a few references to fasting in this book. Certain people should never fast: pregnant women, the sick, those with diabetes and certain other medical conditions. Before fasting, check with your Physician first,
to learn if this is something you can safely do.

ISBN 13: 978-0-9995307-6-4

Preston, S.G., 1951-

PrayerFoundation Evangelical Lay Monks ™
Answers to Prayer
A Global 24-Hr. Prayerchain Since 2000

Includes:
Recommended Books, Recommended Films

1. Prayer. 2. Celtic Christianity. 3. New Monasticism.
4. Christian History. 5. Evangelicals. 6. Threefold Daily Prayers.

Published by: *PrayerFoundation Press* ™
Vancouver, WA 98687

Email: monks@prayerfoundation.org

Books by S.G. Preston

PrayerFoundation Evangelical Lay Monks ™
Series:

Prayer as a Total Lifestyle:
Learning from the Greatest Lives of Prayer

Prayer as a Celtic Lay Monk:
Learning from Celtic Christian Prayer

Answers to Prayer:
A Global 24-Prayerchain Since 2000

———

These books have been written to inspire and motivate you to draw nearer to God in prayer.

Filled with a selection of the best quotations from some of
The Greatest Lives of Prayer,
they can also be used as a Daily Devotional.

Their extensive Indexes (in the Print Versions) make them useful as Reference Works.

They have been written in a clear, concise, easily understood style to make them suitable as a thoughtful *"prayer encouragement"* gift for friends, relatives, and young people.

———

Learning from the Greatest Lives of Prayer:

"Prayer is the helpless and needy child crying to the compassion of the Father's ear and the bounty of a Father's hand."

"God shapes the world by prayer."

"The story of every great Christian achievement is the history of answered prayer."

-E.M. Bounds (1835-1913)

Dedicated to:

Lewis W. Preston

My earthly Father,
who did so much for me.

Who did so much for so many others:
fighting across the Pacific to Japan,
in the Navy during World War II.

I honor you, and your Service.

———

Our Mission:

*"To Promote Prayer Among All Christians
and Proclaim Christ to the World."*

———

Scripture Basis:

*"But we will devote ourselves continually to prayer,
and to the ministry of the word."*

-Acts 6:4

Contents:

6. *The LORD That Heals* (*Yahweh Rapha*)

7. *The Everlasting God* (*El Olam*)

8. *The LORD Our Righteousness* (*Yahweh Tsidkenu*)

*"Ever since I became a Christian
I have thought that the best, perhaps the only,
service I could do for my unbelieving neighbours
was to explain and defend
the belief that has been common
to nearly all Christians at all times."*

-C.S. Lewis (1898-1963)
From: *Mere Christianity*

Dear *PrayerFoundation* ™

"Behold how good and how pleasant it is,
for brethren to dwell together in unity."

-Psalm 133:1

Dear friends, Grace, peace, strength and joy to you in Christ Jesus! Just a note to say I enjoyed visiting your website today! Joined with you in seeking first Jesus and His kingdom,

-Gary P. Bergel (President, *Intercessors for America*)

Just scanned through your site and it looks great. Really interesting too, that you allow women monks. Did you read about our *'boiler rooms'*? These are urban monastic communities but with a slight difference. We took some of the ideas and added some of our own and came up with these communities. I'm really interested in reading about the old *Celtic monks*. I'll put your website up as a link.

-Phil, Webmaster: *24-7 Prayer* (U.K.)

I am writing to (learn who to contact to) request permission to use a photo of *George Müller* **on my website.** Thank you very much,

-Catherine L. Evans, Founder, President: *Orphanages for Africa*

Thanks for your help.

Regards, -Shane B.; Principal, *Ministry Training College* (Auckland, New Zealand)

June 14, 2006 - Answer to Prayer: Dearly Beloved of The Lord, thank you so much for your prayers, and thank God: in June of '93, they gave an atheist in his hospital room six months to live, and in 2006, I'm born again -- and the Lord added many years to my life. The Lord bless and keep you.

Praying for a good summer for you, -Brother Rick

9

How It All Began

"The joy which answers to prayer give,
cannot be described;
and the impetus which they afford
to the spiritual life
is exceedingly great."

-George Müller (1805-1898)

A Prayer Encouragement Ministry

In March of 1999, my wife Linda and I founded the *PrayerFoundation* ™ and its Lay Monastic Order, the *Knights of Prayer*,™ as the first Evangelical Monastic Order on the Internet; the only one for the next four years.

Nine years later, on February 3, 2008, Religion Historian Molly Worthen, in her article *"In the beginning...,"* would write in the Boston Globe:

"Vancouver, Wash.-based evangelicals S.G. Preston and his wife, Linda, were inspired to found their monastic order, the Knights of Prayer, after visits to Ireland and Assisi, Italy, the home of St. Francis...

...the Prestons consider their monastic order a "prayer encouragement ministry."

We created a 1,300 webpage website of *"Prayer Teaching & Resources from All Christian Communions and Eras."* This was equivalent to 4,000 printed book pages., or twenty 200-page books.

The website went *viral*, receiving up to 2.4 million page-downloads per month. Nearly 30 million per year. Over *half a billion* page downloads over next twenty years.

Christians in 47 countries joined with us as Members of our *Knights of Prayer Lay Monastic Order.*™

A 24-Hr. Prayerchain

In 2000, we began a *24-Hr. Prayerchain.*™ We received prayer requests daily from all over the world, eventually from eighty-eight different countries, with up to two thousand Christians each year volunteering as *Prayer Warriors* to pray for these prayer requests.

One of the main purposes of the website was to *"encourage prayer among all Christians."* There is nothing more encouraging than reading or hearing about how our loving and merciful God answers the prayers of His people.

Christians let us know both when and how God answered their prayers.

I personally have been extremely blessed by reading through these answers to prayer over the years. I know they will be a blessing to you as well, to the increase of your faith.

God Answers Prayers

You will see many of your own problems and concerns in these prayer requests.

Our God is a God who answers prayer. May these *Answers to Prayer* bless you, and help you grow closer to Christ, as much as they have myself and Linda.

May they greatly *encourage* you in your *prayer life.*

Yours in Christ,

-S.G. Preston

Lay Monk Preston
Vancouver, Washington
St. Patrick's Day
March 17, 2021

Prayer & Christ's Great Commission

*"The man or woman at home who prays
often has as much to do with the effectiveness
of the missionary on the field, and consequently
with the results of his or her labors, as the missionary."*

-R. A. Torrey (1856-1928) Successor to:
Dwight Moody's Ministry of Worldwide Evangelism

———

"The Cross is not just a message. It is a way of life."
"The history of missions is the history of answered prayer."

-Samuel Zwemer (1867-1952) *"Apostle to Islam"*

———

**"In no other way can the believer become as fully involved
with God's work, especially the work of world evangelism,
as in intercessory prayer."**

-Dick Eastman (President: *Every Home for Christ*
and *America's National Prayer Committee*)

———

*"We can reach our world if we will.
The greatest lack today is not people or funds.
The greatest need is prayer."*

-Wesley Duewel (1916-2016) Missionary to India
President: OMS *International (One Mission Society)*

———

*"There are three stages to every great work of God;
first it is impossible, then it is difficult, then it is done."*

-Hudson Taylor (1832-1905)
Founder: *China Inland Mission*

* * *

1. *The LORD My Shepherd (Yahweh Shammah)*

1.1 Mind Restored, Surgery Canceled, God's Clear Direction

*"Whenever God determines to do a great work,
He first sets His people to pray."*

-Charles Spurgeon (1834-1892)

———

*"We do not make requests of You because we are righteous,
but because of Your great mercy."*

-Daniel 9:18

Dec. 4, 2000 - Urgent Prayer Request:

Please pray for my niece, Allison; she is only five years old. A rock came through the windshield of the car she was riding in, and struck her in the eye.

-Tom (Washington State)

Answer to Prayer - Feb. 6, 2001

My niece Allison got to go home at Christmastime. The Doctors did not think she would regain mental awareness and physical ability, that her mind was gone. *They thought wrong!* Allison is 90% back to normal. She has learned to walk, and talk, and eat on her own again. She still needs some work with talking, but as far as we are concerned, she is doing wonderfully.

I truly think God has his eye on Allison. She is a wonderful person and we are all so glad that we can share our lives with her. I wanted to thank you for all your prayers. At this point the Doctors have given Allison a clean bill of health.

-Tom (Washington State)

Apr. 8, 2001 - Answer to Prayer:

First of all, thanks for all the prayers. Friday night almost ended 12 years of a devoted marriage. We had actually decided to call it quits; at least that's what she said she wanted. With everybody's prayers, we are now going to try to work things out again. Thanks so much for all the prayer support.

Apr. 30, 2001 - Urgent Prayer Request:

Hello. My name is Caroline. My father is going to have open-heart surgery this Thursday. Would you please say a prayer for him? I just cannot imagine life without him. He has been the greatest dad that anyone could ever ask for. We've been through some tough times together.

My mother left us back in 1991. It was a hard time. Us kids would rebel and take our anger out on him for her leaving. I myself always ran away when I just couldn't take the pressure anymore. But my dad never gave up on us. He continued to work to put us through Catholic high school. I am now 27 years old. I just need extra prayers for him to make it through this ordeal. I really appreciate your help. Thank you so much. Love,

-Caroline

Answer to Prayer - May 2, 2001 (Two Days Later.)

Dear Lay Monk Preston & family, I want to thank everyone from the bottom of my heart for your gracious prayers. My dad is doing fine now. He went to the hospital today to get a catheterization done to clear up his arteries. Now the doctors said that he does not need the open-heart surgery tomorrow!!

THANK GOD!!!!! He is a miracle worker!!! Today was a total blessing. Now my dad has to just recover from today's minor surgery. I'm sure that'll go well, too. He is a very strong person. Again, I want to thank all of you for your love and support. Sincerely,

-Caroline

June 3, 2001 - Answer to Prayer:

Just arrived home, the surgery I was talking about lately was finished. Thank you for your prayers. During the surgery itself I didn't feel any anxiety.

I received much mail from friends. Even my letter to the Pope was answered (thanks for your prayers). My friend passed his law exam (thanks also).

June 6, 2001 - Answer to Prayer:

Praise His holy name, Lord we praise You, You are so wonderful and awesome, and we thank You again that You always answer our prayers. I asked my brothers and sisters to pray with me for some clear directions and glory to God; as always, He answered! I sincerely thank you from the bottom of my heart for your kind letters and words of encouragement.

I thank you and I love you, for you've been a family to me. -N.

July 7, 2001 - Answer to Prayer:

Thanks for praying for my Aunt. She went home from the hospital this past Monday, after 45 days in the hospital. They told her when she first came in, that they only gave her a 5% chance to live.

June 13, 2001 - Answer to Prayer:

I wrote a couple of months ago to put my brother Domenic's name on your prayer line. He had, just days before, been diagnosed with stage 4 small type Cancer. His body was filled with deadly tumors and the hospital personnel felt he would not make the weekend.

There were so many large tumors in his brain, that he was unaware of what was going on. We asked for aggressive Rx. We knew we needed a miracle. They did Radiation and Chemo.

We also got the gift of the heavens. Everyone Prayed!!!!

He came home about two weeks ago and his MRI yesterday shows an 85-90% shrinkage of the tumors in his brain. He will still need more Chemo, etc.

There is no doubt in my mind, that Jesus carried my brother through this tough time. Praise God! Thank you, Jesus!

Thanks to all of you, too, for your prayers, -Carol

Bless the LORD, O my soul;
and all that is within me,
bless His holy name.

Bless the LORD, O my soul,
and do not forget all His benefits:

who forgives all your iniquities;
who heals all your diseases;
who redeems your life from destruction;
who crowns you with lovingkindness and tender mercies,
who satisfies your mouth with good things,
so that your youth is renewed like the eagle's.

The LORD has prepared His throne in the heavens,
and His kingdom rules over all.

Bless the LORD, you His angels;
that excel in strength,
that do His commandments,
hearkening to the sound of His voice.

Bless the LORD, all you His Hosts;
you ministers of His, that do His pleasure.

Bless the LORD,
all His works
in all the places of His dominion.

Bless the LORD, O my soul.

-Psalm 103:1-5; 19-22

16

1.2 Not Cancer, Received Custody, Marriage Restored

"Prayer is the greatest of all forces, because it honors God and brings Him into active aid."

-E.M. Bounds (1835-1913)

———

"What man is there among you, who if his son asks for bread, will give him a stone? Or if he asks for a fish, will give him a serpent?

If you then, being evil, know how to give good gifts to your children, how much more shall your Father who is in heaven, give good things to those that ask Him?"

-Matthew 7:7-11

June 17, 2001 - Urgent Prayer Request:

A friend of mine took their six year old daughter to the Doctor on Thursday for headaches. They found a large tumor on her brain. She has to have emergency surgery on Tuesday, 6/19/01. She has only been given a 50% chance of surviving the surgery and then only five years maximum, to live.

Please pray for her. I know miracles happen. She is only six years old; her name is Stephanie.

Answer to Prayer - June 21, 2001 (Four Days Later.)

Just wanted to let you know a miracle has occurred. Stephanie's brain tumor was removed and to their amazement it was not cancerous. *They told them there was only a 1 percent chance of this happening. PRAISE THE LORD!!!!!!*

She will be removed from ICU tomorrow. She is already up and alert, and aware of her surroundings!!!

June 23, 2001 - Answer to Prayer:

A couple weeks ago I sent an email and asked you to pray for me in regard to my long term disability.

I would like for you to know that I received a letter yesterday telling me that the decision had been in my favor and everything would be okay.

I want to first thank my Lord and Master for keeping me in the hollow of His hands, and blessing me with this answer of prayer.

Next, I want everyone to know just how much I appreciate you for taking your time to pray for me and to keep praying for me until an answer came through. I know God will bless every one of you in a very special way. Thank you from the bottom of my heart for you and your prayers.

God Bless and keep you. -Margie

_____

June 23, 2001 - Answer to Prayer:

I am losing a little weight, and that is great. Also, the depression is getting a tiny bit better! God is drawing me closer to him through all this, and I pray He is doing the same for Kevin.

Praise God! I know He will come through for us! -Kimberly

_____

June 23, 2001 - Answer to Prayer:

Dear Lay Monk Preston, I have a testimony. Your prayers for my father were answered. He feels better. We have also received direction for our move to the Northeast U.S.

I want to thank all of you. -Peter J.

_____

*"Then you will call upon Me,
and come and pray to Me,
and I will listen to you."*

-Jeremiah 29:12

18

June 29, 2001 - Answer to Prayer:

Thank you for your prayers and thoughts.

My three granddaughters have been returned to my custody and it looks like its permanent this time.

I know it was through the grace of *God* that the situation was turned around, and I thank you so much for your prayers.

-Patricia B.

July 5, 2001 - Prayer Request:

Please continue to pray for Di. When things seem to improve, she relapses. She is full of anger among the panic, anxiety etc. I give her space, but it is not moving along.

Pray that all her anxiety, depression and anger be relieved, and she return home to build our marriage in Christ. It is a spiritual problem that is out of man's hands. Only almighty God can solve this.

Your brother in Christ, -Doug

Answer to Prayer - July 7, 2001 (Two Days Later.)

Di told me she loves me, and believes all her problems are being solved by a strong faith in God, and Jesus in her heart. Her panic, depression and anxiety have subsided.

She has returned to Christ. Your prayers and God's work have performed a miracle.

Answer to Prayer Update - July 9, 2001 (Two More Days Later.)

My miracle is complete, praise God. We found a church family, she has agreed to move home, and we are going to build our marriage in Christ.

God bless all who have prayed. I won't forget my promise to God, or my obligation to the *PrayerFoundation*.™

Your brother in Christ, -Doug

July 23, 2001 - Answer to Prayer:

God has turned my life (and my family's lives) so far around. There was a time we felt hopeless, and our lives were overcome with poverty, pain and suffering.

God opened doors, blessed abundantly, and kept us through it all. I have recently graduated law school, and am sitting for the bar exam in two states.

July 27, 2001 - Answer to Prayer:

Thank you for praying for my mother, for she definitely improved when I went to see her last week.

-Richard

A Song of Ascents.

**I will lift up my eyes to the hills;
where does my help come from?**

My help comes from the LORD,
who made heaven and earth.

He will not allow your foot to be moved;
He who protects you will not slumber.
Behold! He who protects Israel shall neither slumber nor sleep.

The LORD is your protector.
The LORD is your shade at your right hand.
The sun shall not smite you by day, nor the moon by night.

**The LORD shall preserve you from all evil.
He shall preserve your soul.**

The LORD shall preserve your going out and your coming in
from this time forward, forever and ever.

-Psalm 121

1.3 Successful Surgery, Classes Passed, Seeing Progress

"A young monk asked Abba Macarius,

'How should we pray?'

The elderly monk answered,

*'You do not need to pray long prayers.
Just lift up your hands and pray:*

*'Lord, Your will be done,
You know my needs, have mercy on me.'*

*And if the struggle becomes even more fierce,
pray: 'Lord, help me!'*

*God is well aware of our needs,
and always shows us
His great mercy.'"*

-Sayings of the Desert Fathers (c. 300 A.D.)

———

*"Whatever you shall ask in My Name, that will I do,
that the Father may be glorified in the Son.*

If you shall ask anything in My Name, I will do it."

-John 14:13-14

July 28, 2001 - Answer to Prayer:

Thanking God and thanks for your prayers. My prayers have been answered. My surgery went O.K. I got exemptions for my ROTC training. I really hoped for this, and I really didn't think it was possible; but it happened. Wow!

Thanks and God bless. What would I do without your prayers? God is really answering my prayers through your intercessions.

-(Philippines)

July 31, 2001 - Urgent Prayer Request:

Please pray for Dad, he is having triple bypass surgery, tomorrow. It is a serious surgery, and he has 50% chance of surviving. Only has 30% of heart functioning, all three major arteries are blocked. He has congestive heart failure. Thank You, so much for your prayers, *Everyone!*

God Bless You! Jesus' Love, -Lynsley <>< (Florida)

Answer to Prayer - Aug. 1, 2001 (The Next Day.)

I Have A Praise Report! Thank you, so much for your prayers. My Dad is doing great from his surgery. Everything went well. He did have a bad time; could not breathe on his own; but today, August 1, they took him off the respirator and other machines, and he was able to talk today.

Praise God, and Thank You, for all the beautiful prayers from all the *Prayer Warriors*, and the *PrayerFoundation*.™ God Bless You!

Jesus' Love, -Lynsley <>< (Florida)

August 2, 2001 - Answer to Prayer:

I want to say thank you for all of the prayers for my children / family and to share praises of answered prayers. My son Sean and my daughter Lauren, both passed their summer school classes and are back on track...Thank you Lord!!!

I am also not feeling so defeated by my teens and their problems. :) Our older son Ryan (age 19) said that he opened his Bible last week...progress. He says that he will sign up for college and get a job.

Thank you again, :) -Linda (California)

"He is, he sees, he loves: the eternity of God is his life, the truth of God is his light, the goodness of God is his joy."

-St. Augustine of Hippo (354-430 A.D.)

August 2, 2001 - Answer to Prayer:

Thank you for all your prayers for my son Steve and his tests. He came home very discouraged after he took the tests and said he felt he did not pass. He got the results yesterday and passed his math course with a B. This is the third time he repeated this course. I know God answered your and my prayers.

-Thank you, God; and thank you, friends, for your prayers.

July 28, 2001 - Urgent Prayer Request:

In need of urgent prayer for T.C., a 13 year old boy who has been on a self-destructive path since Aug. of 2000. He's had hospitalizations, and is on lots of medication. Please pray for God to take authority over his mind and for Him to fill T.C. up with His presence and love. Hoping for placement in a group home to stabilize him, but only if it is God's will. We need a miracle, or miracles, for every problem he faces.

Thank you for caring and prayers; without them T.C. is not going to make it. -Joyce

Answer to Prayer - August 4, 2001 (One Week Later.)

Thank you for your prayers for our 13 year-old grandson. God is moving. T.C. saw a spiritual counselor this week, and asked for prayer for God to make a way for this to continue with Pastor R.

Also, he was accepted into a group home on a trial basis. -Joyce

---

August 23, 2001 - Answer to Prayer:

John S. was transported by Life Flight to the Hospital. Surgery on his arm was successful and he has feeling in 4 fingers.

God is Good. Thanks, -Don <><

---

*"Create in me a clean heart, O God,
and renew a right spirit within me."* -Psalm 51:10

23

August 9, 2001 - Answer to Prayer:

Thank all of you wonderful *Prayer Warriors* for your prayers for my grandson, Caleb. He is doing so much better now, even though the Doctors never did find out what was wrong with him.

But that does not really matter; the only thing that matters is that *God* heard our prayers and answered them.

Again, thank you for all your prayers...

-Margie

A Psalm of David.
When he fled from Absalom, his son.

LORD, how they are increased that trouble me!
Many are those that rise up against me.
Many there are, that say of my soul:
"There is no help for him from God." Selah.

But You, O LORD, are a shield for me:
my glory, and the lifter up of my head.
I cried out to the LORD with my voice,
and He heard me from His holy hill. Selah.

I lay myself down and slept.
I awoke, for the LORD protected me.
I will not be afraid of ten thousand people,
who have set themselves against me all around.

Arise, O LORD! Save me, O my God.

You have struck all my enemies on the cheekbone.
You have broken the teeth of the ungodly.

Salvation belongs to the LORD.
Your blessing rests upon Your people. Selah.

-Psalm 3

1.4 Job Obtained, Depression Gone, Kidneys Healing

"The Christian life is not a constant high.
I have my moments of deep discouragement.
I have to go to God in prayer with tears in my eyes,
and say 'O God, forgive me.'
Or 'Help me.'"

-Billy Graham (1918-2018)

———

"Be anxious for nothing,
but in everything by prayer and supplication
with thanksgiving, let your requests
be made known to God.

And the peace of God,
which passes all understanding,
shall keep your hearts and minds
through Christ Jesus."

-Philippians 4:6-7

August 9, 2001 - Answer to Prayer:

On July 22nd my father had a heart attack.

The first scheduled operation (right after I posted a prayer request) was rescheduled when a physician's assistant discovered he had been given a blood thinner upon admittance, that had to be weaned from his body, or else he could have hemorrhaged.

The operation was rescheduled for a few days later and he started to complain of a sore throat but no one discovered anything unusual until the anesthesiologist couldn't properly insert the breathing tube.

A specialist discovered he had an allergic reaction to a potassium pill he was given earlier in the week, and his throat was severely inflamed. It would have been a danger in trying to remove the tube after surgery.

Both times, just at the right moment, discoveries were made that, had they not been made, could have caused serious complications for him.

A quadruple bypass was performed a week ago. He was physically ready for it and came thru with minor complications and is coming home today. My father has been given a new lease on life, and has a healthy 20-year span ahead, God willing.

I know it was the prayers that stopped the first two operations and I know it was your prayers that pulled him through, and brought him home. I will be forever grateful to all of you and the Lord Jesus Christ, because my dad is my best friend, and my life wouldn't be the same without him.

I have also signed up as a *Prayer Warrior* as well. Thank you, and I hope this inspires others to see that prayer does work, and if it is God's will, then whatever you pray for will be.

We left it to God, who decided the fate of the operation and my dad's health; and I guess God saw he had a lot of people rooting for his life here on earth, so he gave him to us for a little while longer.

-Thank you, and to God be all the glory...Amen.

August 16, 2001 - Answer to Prayer:

I am happy to announce...I have obtained a job in radio sales, with the potential to make enough to feed and support my family. Thank you all for your prayers; y'all work miracles together!! God Bless You all!

But things are looking up. We have groceries, and a little money to buy school clothes for my girls. God is *Good!*

Thank you all for being there for us. -C., J.M., B., T., C.

"For your Maker is your husband; the Lord of Hosts is His name;
and your Redeemer the Holy One of Israel;
the God of the whole earth shall He be called."

-Isaiah 54:5

26

August 21, 2001 - Answer to Prayer:

The Lord has totally taken away all of my Depression! I had it for several months. The Lord also today took care of my financial problems by giving me a wonderful job! All Glory to God, and my thanks to all of you *Prayer Warriors* who have been praying for me.

All Praise to Jesus! -G.

August 24, 2001 - Urgent Prayer Request:

Please pray for my nephew Tommy. He was just diagnosed with failing kidneys. This came on so suddenly, they don't even know what caused it. He is just 20.

Answer to Prayer - August 30, 2001 (Six Days Later.)

Thank you so much for your prayers. Tommy went home today from the hospital and even though he has a long recovery (about 6 months) ahead of him, the doctors feel that the tubular necrosis that caused his kidney damage will regenerate. God bless you all, and once again, thank you for your prayers. Our good Lord promised that when two or more gathered together to pray, that He too would be there. Forever in Christ.

Sept. 12, 2001 - Answer to Prayer:

Dear Lay Monks at Prayer, I requested prayer for a visit to my family a couple of weeks ago. I had many fears. I am thanking you for your prayers, and reporting they were answered in a miraculous way. I didn't want to leave them, and we really did all enjoy our time together in a very honest, not superficial way. I felt so at home and comfortable there. They have changed and done "their work" on themselves, in their own way.

Thank you and blessings to you and yours. -D.

"O LORD, open my lips, and my mouth shall declare Your praise."

-Psalm 51:15

Sept. 18, 2001 - Answer to Prayer:

My prayers have been continually answered. I do thank the Creator for those answered prayers.

My son seems to be safe, I am striving for improvement, and God is continually blessing. I see the blessing in all things. This, I know, is a *testimony*. I do thank Him. I believe the *24-Hr. Prayers* are the main factor in keeping peace.

Brothers and Sisters, I know that prayer works. -Robert

"And Elijah arrived at a cave, and lodged there;
and, behold; the word of the LORD came to him,
and God said to him:

'What are you doing here, Elijah?'

And Elijah answered,
'I have been very jealous for the LORD God of Hosts:
for the children of Israel have forsaken Your covenant,
thrown down Your altars,
and slain your prophets with the sword;
and I, even I only am left,
and they seek my life, to take it away.'

And God said:
'Go, and stand upon the mountain before the LORD.'

And behold, the LORD passed by,
and a mighty wind rent the mountains,
and broke in pieces the rocks before the LORD,
but the LORD was not in the earthquake.

And after the earthquake a fire,
but the LORD was not in the fire;
and after the fire,

a still, small voice."

-1 Kings 19:9-13

1.5 *Prayer Warrior* Comments

Dear Lay Monk Preston, thank you for responding to my letter. I never expected for you to e-mail back. This world has become so hardened, I never take anything for granted.

I want to think you for your prayers, and thank all the *Prayer Warriors* and everyone else that is praying for me...*I really do need it,* or I would have never written to you.

I will keep Lay Monk Danny in my prayers....I prayed for all the *Prayer Requests* on your Site, and will continue to do so...all those people are in desperate need of prayer and miracles.

May God bless you *all* and keep you all in *His* care!! -Fran

---

Dear Brother (and Sister) Lay Monks of *PrayerFoundation,*™ one time I wrote to an organization requesting prayer for my chronic pain. Since then I started receiving letters and requests for prayer for others.

I must tell you that it's like an elixir to my body and soul, when in pain I sit in front of my computer and read of the misery that so many people are living in. The pain of terrible diseases, and the heartbreak of many parents because of their ungrateful and heartless children. I am very committed to this work, in many ways.

First, it helps me to realize that there are people who are much worse off than I am; in more pain, with broken bodies and souls. Secondly; I forget the "Me" that is in the way of being a good Christian, and instead console and comfort the sad and poor of spirit.

Respectfully yours, -Ana (One of your *Prayer Warriors*)

"The LORD is good to those that wait for Him;
to those that seek Him.

It is good to both hope in,
and to wait quietly for the LORD."

-Lamentations 3:25-26

1.6 Apostle to Ireland, Missionary to India & Persia

Apostle to Ireland

*"For daily I expect to be murdered or betrayed
or reduced to slavery if the occasion arises.*

*But I fear nothing, because of the promises of Heaven;
for I have cast myself into the hands of Almighty God,
who reigns everywhere."*

*"I pray to God to give me perseverance, and to deign that I be a
faithful witness to Him to the end of my life for my God."*

-St. Patrick (386-461 A.D.)

Missionary to India & Persia

Henry Martyn arrived in India in April 1806, where he preached and translated the whole of the New Testament into Urdu, Persian, and Judaeo-Persic. He also translated the Psalms into Persian and the *Book of Common Prayer* into Urdu. From India, he set out for Persia (today's Iran). Martyn was seized with fever, and though the plague was raging at Tokat, he was forced to stop there, unable to continue. He went home to be with the Lord on October 16th, 1812.

*"Let me burn out for God.
After all, whatever God may appoint, prayer is the great thing.
Oh, that I might be a man of prayer."*

-Henry Martyn (1781-1812) Missionary
Anglican Priest (Died from Plague at age 31)

---

*"For I know that my Redeemer lives, and that He shall stand in
the last days upon the earth; and though my body be destroyed,
yet in my flesh I shall see God: who I shall see for myself,
and my eyes shall behold, and not another."*

-Job 19:25-27

1.7 Dear *PrayerFoundation* ™

My name is Jay L*** and I'm a reporter for Associated Press. I'm working on a story on those who are praying for...our soldiers, or any other aspect of the current war. I want to ask specifically about the power of prayer and its importance in the midst of this conflict. Please e-mail me or call **** if you have a moment to talk.

Thanks for any time you can give me. -Jay L.

Mabuhay & Merry Christmas from the Philippines! Wishing you all the best and thanking you for your undoubting prayers for me and those I hold dear.

God bless you this Christmas, -Francis (Philippines)

Dear friends, Thanks for your love and prayers.

God bless you. -Evangelist Pervaz M. (Pakistan)

Your website made me feel like rejoicing. I have always felt that God wanted me to learn much of what is revealed in learning how to live a life of prayer.

Yet I have found little to nothing in the way of guidelines on how to start, even though I grew up in church.

-(Korea)

"Blessed is the man that walks not in the counsel of the ungodly, nor stands in the way of sinners, nor sits in the seat of the scornful; but his delight is in the Law of the LORD, and in His Law, he meditates day and night.

And he shall be like a tree, planted by the rivers of water, that brings forth his fruit in its season. His leaf also shall not wither, and whatever he does shall prosper."

-Psalm 1:1-3

A ground-breaking ministry...just beautiful to see your heart and vision. I would truly love to become involved. I see your ministry as having potential to meet a very specific need at this moment in Evangelical Christendom. I commend you for your steps of faith. As a Southern Baptist pastor who loves the writings of John Piper, C. S. Lewis, and Charles Spurgeon, and who also has a deep appreciation for Celtic Christianity... I will pray for you and your ministry. I really love your website. I really feel a peace and happiness just reading everything. Your ministry has been ministering to me and I'm just thankful.

Thanks for being there. Love in Christ, -Dave (Tennessee)

Dear Brothers and Sisters of Prayer, I have been surfing your Site and am delighted that someone has started a monastic order that is non-denominational, Spirit-filled, and based solely on God's Holy word.

The life of Francis is so inspiring to so many, that His radical discipleship of our Lord is contagious and crosses denominational lines. It is a blessing to see that you have blended traditional monasticism with solid Reformed doctrine. What a perfect match.

There is so much value in a disciplined Christian life. The lukewarm church of our day needs to see anointed men and women of God, filled with the Holy Spirit, living a consecrated life and burning with passion for Christ and His word, and bringing the Kingdom to the lost. These are powerful days to live for Christ, my brethren. I encourage you to stay your course and continue in the Spirit of humility. Continue being strong witnesses for our Lord. People want to see sold out believers who take their call seriously.

I know many evangelicals do not understand why you have gone monastic. I believe that God is restoring the monastic lifestyle in His Church. Blending the Daily Office with contemporary worship. The old with the new. The best of both worlds. Please keep me in your prayers as I will keep you in mine.

May the Lord give you all peace! -Thom

32

What I liked most about your Site was its simplicity. That it was humble, simple and challenging to me to forsake worldly things to do the Lord's will...

-(Munster, Ireland)

"Make your people known for the unity and profession of their faith. Inspire the hearts of your people with your word and teaching.
You called us to preach the Gospel of Your Christ, and to encourage them to lives and works pleasing to You. However tired and physically worn out I am, I will go with joy to that land; with joy I depart for the sake of the Christian faith."

-St. Cyril (826-869 A.D.)
With his brother, St. Methodius: *"Apostles to the Slavs"*

———

"Be great in small things."
"When trying to evangelize, no tool is more effective than that of personal witness. People can argue with points of doctrine, but no one can argue with a personal testimony!"

"Lord, I am here! What do you want me to do?"
"Here I am, Lord, send me; send me to the ends of the earth; send me to the rough, the savage pagans of the wilderness; send me from all that is called...earthly comfort; send me to death itself, if it be but in Your service, and to promote Your kingdom."

-St. Frances Xavier (1506-1552) *"Apostle to Japan"*

———

"The spirit of Christ is the spirit of missions.
The nearer we get to Him, the more intensely missionary we become."

-Henry Martyn (1781-1812) *"Apostle to India and Persia"*

33

1.8 Abba Nilus, Abba Poemon, St. John Cassian, & St. Augustine of Hippo

"Abba Nilus said:
'Do not be always wanting everything to turn out
as you think it should, but rather as God pleases,
then you will be undisturbed and thankful in your prayer.'"

"Abba Poemen taught:
'Do not give your heart to that which does not satisfy your heart.'"

-Sayings of the Desert Fathers (c. 300 A.D.)

———

"It is useless to boast of fasting, vigils, and reading of Scripture,
when we have not achieved love for God and for our fellow man."

-St. John Cassian (c. 360-c. 345 A.D.)
Author: *The Conferences* and *The Institutes*

———

"At the beginning of the conversation,
Jesus did not make Himself known to her.
First she caught sight of a thirsty man, then a Jew,
then a Rabbi, afterwards a Prophet, last of all the Messiah.

She tried to get the better of the thirsty man,
she showed dislike of the Jew, she heckled the Rabbi,
she was swept off her feet by the Prophet,
and she adored the Christ."

-St. Ephrem the Syrian (c. 306-373 A.D.)

———

"Many times have I spoken and regretted it,
but silence I never regretted."

-St. Augustine of Hippo (354-430 A.D.)
Author: *Confessions* and *The City of God*

* * *

1.9 Lay Monk Thoughts:
Pray Without Ceasing

*"...He is not far from any one of us;
for in Him we live, and move, and have our being."*

-Acts 17: 27-28

"God is Omnipresent: He is always present with us. We know this truth intellectually, but we may live as though it was not a reality. To *"practice the presence of God"* is to be in constant awareness of God's presence.

It is to be in constant communion with God, in a constant state of prayer. The awareness of God's presence that we experience when we pray, is the awareness we need to cultivate at all times. This is *"prayer without ceasing."* 1 Thessalonians 5:16-18 teaches:

"Rejoice always. Pray without ceasing. In everything give thanks. For this is the will of God in Christ Jesus concerning you." We find an example of this in the life of Brother Lawrence (1614-1691):

**"That his prayer was nothing else but a sense
of the presence of God, his soul being at that time
insensible to everything but Divine love:**

*and that when the appointed times of prayer were past,
he found no difference, because he still continued with God,
praising and blessing Him with all His might,
so that he passed his life in continual joy..."*

-From the book: *The Practice of the Presence of God
by Brother Lawrence*

———

*"And the smoke of the incense,
intermingled with the prayers of the saints,
ascended up before God
from the angel's hand."*

-Revelation: 8:4

* * *

2. *The LORD is Peace (Yahweh Shalom)*

2.1 No Cancer, Awoke from Coma, Money Received

"God is not looking for men of great faith,
He is looking for common men to trust His great faithfulness."

-Hudson Taylor (1832-1905) Founder: *China Inland Mission*

———

"Therefore I say to you: whatever things you desire, when you pray,
believe that you receive them, and you shall have them."

-Mark 11:24

Sept. 22, 2001 - Answer to Prayer:

Just wanted to announce in joy that our mother has learned that she has no Cancer. We thank you for helping in prayers, it was really a moving experience.

Thanks. -(Philippines)

———

Oct. 21, 2001 - Answer to Prayer:

Many of you have been praying for my mother, Cecelia. The most recent procedure she had on her heart seems to have been a success...the bleeding stopped. It's a good thing she was receiving prayer. My Aunt Geordina, who had the brain tumor removed, is doing as well as can be expected. It is truly a miracle that she awoke from the coma. She is able to feed herself, and speak slowly...

Thank you, -Lay Monk Christine (Hawaii)

———

"But to the Son He said, 'Your throne, O God, is forever and ever...'"

-Ephesians 1:8

"For in Christ dwells all the fullness of the Deity, in bodily form."

-Colossians 2:9

Oct. 22, 2001 - Answer to Prayer:

I have to thank you for your love and prayers. I see miracles every day, and it is through prayer. I have asked for help with my finances, and a friend sent me $180.00 today...that helped so much. God bless you all.

Jesus Adores You, -Lynn (Jeremiah 33:3)

Oct. 22, 2001 - Answer to Prayer:

Dear Prayer Warriors, My little grandson Nicco, 4 1/2 years old, was diagnosed with an inoperable brainstem tumor in November of 99, just two months before he turned 3. After 11 months of heavy chemo, he could not even walk. At this point the doctors were worried the tumor was growing again, and put him on 6 weeks of radiation. A month later when he had his next MRI the doctors realized that the tumor had been shrinking all along. They say they cannot explain this.

But we know that all the prayers for Nicco have been heard, and that is why the tumor has shrunk.

Thank you and God bless you all. -Thordis

Oct. 27, 2001 - Answer to Prayer:

Dear Special Prayer Family, I have to tell the good news before I ask for more prayer for others and myself....I was very surprised to get a loan at college that was a lot more than what I expected....It helped me pay rent and I feel peace instead of stress....

Thank You Lord, and thank you Prayer Warriors...but *Praise The Lord* and thank you so much for your prayer ministry. -Lynn

---

"One thing have I desired of the LORD, that will I seek after; that I may dwell in the House of the LORD all the days of my life, to behold the beauty of the LORD, and to enquire in His Temple."

-Psalm 27:4

37

Oct. 20, 2001 - Prayer Request:

Dear *Prayer Warriors*, Please pray that God would help to strengthen me against this terrible depression and suicidal feelings that I have been battling. I am feeling so spiritually attacked. Some days are just so difficult as the physical pain is just so bad and just goes on and on.

Please pray that God would heal me. -J. (New Zealand)

Answer to Prayer - Oct. 21, 2001 (One Day Later.)

Thank you so much for praying for me. I haven't felt any pain today and haven't taken any painkillers. Although I am a little washed out and tired, I can really feel God's peace and joy. It is a miracle for me to be physically feeling this good.

The depression appears to be really lifting and I feel like I can face tomorrow with courage and trust in God. -J. (New Zealand)

Answer to Prayer Update - Oct. 30, 2001 (Nine Days Later.)

Dear *Prayer Warriors*, I really praise God, that he is keeping the physical pain I've been battling long term, at bay. The prayers for release from pain and depression are working.

God is so faithful and awesome. -J. (New Zealand)

Oct. 31, 2001 - Answer to Prayer:

I thank God for the miracle that has happened in my life; that I have been admitted to Tennessee State University.

-Kenny

"For as the heaven is high above the earth,
so great is His mercy toward those that reverence Him.
As far as the east is from the west,
so far has He removed our transgressions from us."

-Psalm 103:11-12

S.G. Preston

Oct. 28, 2001 - Prayer Request:

I am requesting a prayer for a good friend, T., whose mother just had back surgery, and is in need of prayers for healing. T.'s mother's name is Sonny, and she is in her 70's.

Thank you. -Mark

Answer to Prayer - Nov. 1, 2001

Thank you for praying for Sonny! I just heard she is getting better, so there was an answer to prayer!

God bless! -Mark

"For My thoughts are not your thoughts,
neither are your ways My ways, says the LORD.

For as the heavens are higher than the earth,
so are My ways higher than your ways,
and My thoughts higher than your thoughts.

For as the rain falls from heaven,
and does not return there; but waters the earth,
and makes it bring forth and bud;
that it may give seed to the sower,
and bread to the eater,

so shall My word be that goes forth out of My mouth:
it shall not return to Me empty,
but it shall accomplish that which I please,
and it shall accomplish the purpose I intended.

For you shall go out with joy,
and be led forth with peace;
the mountains and hills shall
break forth before you into singing,
and all the trees of the field
shall clap their hands."

-Isaiah 55:8-12

2.2 Red Tape Gone, Now Have Money, Freed from Taliban

"In prayer, it is better to have a heart without words, than words without a heart."

-John Bunyan (1628-1688)
Author: *Pilgrim's Progress*

———

*"But you, when you pray,
enter into your prayer room,
and when you have shut the door,
pray to your Father, who is unseen;
and your Father, who sees in secret,
shall reward you openly."*

-Matthew 6:6

Oct. 27, 2001 - Prayer Request:

Pray for my son-in-law Erik's marijuana problem...healing in the marriage of Erik and my daughter, Jen. Pray for Jen and Erik going into counseling...please pray for love and peace and a humble spirit and a good counselor... *Praise Jesus, the joy and victory of my heart.*

-Lynn (Washington State)

Answer To Prayer - Nov. 1, 2001 (Five Days Later.)

I have a wonderful answer to prayer, too...My daughter called and she and her husband are going to church this weekend....Erik is humbled by his mistakes and is now open to letting the love of Jesus come in...

My Jen is ecstatic...she is one of the most patient 23 year-olds I know...she and I were separated for 9 years, through a tragic and hurtful experience, but now are reconciled and so happy.

-Lynn (Washington State)

Nov. 4, 2001 - Answer to Prayer

Praise God, for He hears our prayers!!! Just an update on the prayer request I asked for, for my brother Dan: God has answered our prayers, and given Dan an Oncologist who is an advocate for his patients. In one phone call, the red tape blocking the recommended treatment was gone. Dan begins Oral Chemotherapy on Monday, with a very positive outlook. I thank you for all your prayers.

God Bless You!!! -Cindy

Nov. 3, 2001 - Answer to Prayer:

Dear *Prayer Warriors*, I thank all who prayed on behalf of my family. I met with the parenting investigator this past Friday, and he is not only going to give me the bi-weekly visitation I expected, but is also going to recommend that I be allowed to take my children to church with me on Sundays.

Praise God. -F. (Tacoma, Washington)

Nov. 4, 2001 - Answer to Prayer:

Thank you so much for all your prayers. After Mack was put on your *24-Hr. Prayerchain,* his white blood cell count has gone down from over 150,000 to almost 95,000...with only *one* Chemo. treatment given. *According to the Doctors this is incredible!!* But not to any of us who believe.

Praise God for all He has done, and God bless you for the work you do for Him. -Elizabeth

---

Nov. 6, 2001 - Answer to Prayer:

Thank You for praying for us to have a safe flight to Florida and back. We had the best flight ever; it was smooth and the peace of God was with us.

-C.M., D.M.

Nov. 8, 2001 - Answer to Prayer:

Thank you for your prayers. I asked prayer for Terry, who had a tumor. He went to the Doctor, and they could not find anything.

-Thank you, Jesus!

Nov. 10, 2001 - Answer to Prayer:

Just wanted to thank you for your prayers. God is moving! My daughter came up with my grandson, 6 months old this weekend, so I was not lonely. Kari wrote that she is not as depressed, and feeling hope and joy again. I now have money.

You're a Blessing and a Joy, and I Thank You from the Bottom of My Heart. Jesus Always Triumphs...

Prayer Is The Key! -Lynn

Nov. 10, 2001 - Answer to Prayer:

A friend of mine at ***** would probably be interested in your group! -Thank you for your prayers, many have been answered!

Nov. 17, 2001 - Answer to Prayer:

I just wanted to say thank you so much for praying for Dayna and Heather, the two American Christian aid workers in Afghanistan.

Praise God for their freedom! I know Dayna personally and both girls are good friends of my friends. It's really so amazing...

God is so faithful! :) -Allison

Note: Heather and Dayna were held prisoner by the Taliban in Afghanistan.

We had placed them on our *24 -Hr. Prayerchain* for four weeks, at which time the prayers of our thousands of volunteer *Prayer Warriors*, along with the prayers of other Christians from all over the world were answered, and they were released.

S.G. Preston

To the Director of Music: to be played on Gittith
(a stringed instrument of the people of Gath).
A Psalm of David.

O LORD, our Lord;
how excellent is Your name in all the earth!
You have set Your glory above the heavens.

Out of the mouths of children and infants, You have prepared praise.
Because of Your enemies;
that You might silence the enemy, and the avenger.

When I consider Your heavens, the work of Your fingers;
the moon and the stars, which You have created, I wonder:

"What is humanity, that You are mindful of us?"
and, "What is the Son of Man, that You visit Him?"
You made Him for a short time, a little lower than the angels.
Then You crowned Him with glory and honor.
You have given Him dominion over all the works of Your hands.
You have put all things under His feet.

All sheep and oxen. Yes, and the beasts of the field.
The birds of the air, and the fish of the sea,
and whatever passes through the paths of the seas.

O LORD, our Lord;
how excellent is Your name in all the earth!

-Psalm 8

————

"But we see Jesus;
who was made for a short time,
a little lower than the angels;
crowned with glory and honor
because of His suffering in death.

He, by the grace of God,
tasted death for everyone."

-Hebrews 2:9

43

2.3 Tumor Gone, Son Finally Visits, One Day to Live

*"The reason why many fail in battle is because
they wait until the hour of battle.*

*The reason why others succeed
is because they have gained
their victory on their knees,
long before the battle came.*

*Anticipate your battles;
fight them on your knees
before temptation comes,
and you will always
have the victory."*

-R.A. Torrey (1856-1928)

———

*"And when you stand praying, forgive,
if you have anything against anyone;
that your Father, who is in Heaven,
may forgive you your trespasses."*

-Mark 11:25

Nov. 20, 2001 - Answer to Prayer:

Thank you for your continued prayers. We received some good news this past week. On Thursday our Radiology Oncologist read the MRI exams that were taken on Monday, and told us that it did not look like the tumor had returned at this point.

Our faith in the Lord Jesus Christ has been tested and has grown stronger through the first part of this ordeal. We are so thankful to all of you that go before our Lord with our requests. We give all glory to God for the answered prayers so far.

We love you all! -Dan

Nov. 23, 2001 - Answer to Prayer (Four Days Later.)

On Monday, November 19, 2001, I requested prayer for my friend Porky who had brain surgery at 1:00 p.m. that day. It's so wonderful to report the surgery was successful, he is at home for Thanksgiving in the company of family and friends.

I talked with him on the phone today, and he is so emotional about the prayers that went up for him--he wants to thank everyone, and just say God Bless You.

I appreciate the prayers, too; all I did was ask, and they were given. I'll never doubt the power of prayer again! -Praise God!

Nov. 27, 2001 - Answer to Prayer:

I want to thank God for His blessings and all of you wonderful Christians for praying for my family and myself. Our son has visited our home with his children for the first time in five years. It was a gift from heaven.

Bless you all. -Ruth

Nov. 27, 2001 - Answer to Prayer:

My Aunt Esther has liver, bone, and brain Cancer. They have not found the source. She did not have the Chemotherapy, like my Mom, and now is doing so much better. Aunt Esther's Cancer was spreading rapidly, even more than my Mom's.

She has had a turnaround and is improving. Thank you so much for all your prayers. Please continue to pray for Aunt Esther. She is very thin, under 100 pounds. She is home, and is improving, very much. Praise The Lord!

Please pray they find the source of the Cancer. God Bless You! God Bless the *PrayerFoundation*,™ and all the *Prayer Warriors*, and all the Lay Monks. God Bless America!

-Thank you so much for all your prayers.

Nov. 27, 2001 - Urgent Prayer Request:

Please continue to pray for Aunt Esther and my Mom, Helena. Please pray for a miracle in both these sweet ladies. Please pray for God's will for my Mom; for her terminal Cancer. The Doctor has been saying she has days. She is bleeding internally from the chemotherapy. Her body is shutting down. She has liver and bone Cancer.

Answer to Prayer - Nov. 28, 2001 (One Day Later.)

Thank you so very much for all your prayers. My Mom, Helena, has had a turn-around, and is drinking and eating for the first time in six weeks. Praise The Lord! Thank You, Jesus! Thank You All! I really do deeply appreciate everyone at the *PrayerFoundation* ™ for all your support and prayers. It is truly a miracle from *God!*

Thank You Jesus, and all the *Prayer Warriors*, and the Lay Monks. Thank You Jesus, for this Miracle. It is purely miraculous. The Doctor was giving my Mom a day to live (yesterday!). The family was making funeral arrangements. This Tuesday morning, my Mom was talking, and ravenously hungry. She ate today more than she ate in 6 weeks, all together.

Praise Jesus, for He does answer prayers. Amen! Thank You, God for all the Blessings! Thank You, God, for all the Miracles! God Bless Everyone! Have a Wonderful Merry Christmas! God Bless America!

Answer to Prayer - Update Dec. 6, 2001 (One Week Later.)

My Mom has had a *Miracle!* She has been healed from Cancer, and now is being healed from Chemotherapy. Praise The Lord! Thank You, *Jesus!* On Saturday, my Mom is being released from Hospice! Praise God!

It is a miracle, since last week the Doctor said she would not last a day. The family had started to make funeral arrangements. Praise The Lord! It is a *Miracle!!!! Jesus Still Heals!!!!!!!!!!!* It is eight days since the Doctor said that. Praise *God!!!!!!!!!!!!!!!*

S.G. Preston

Dec. 4, 2001 - Answer to Prayer:

Dear Brothers and Sisters in Christ...at birth they gave Teaghan a day or two at most to live. He was full term, and a very robust 6 lbs., but there was a serious problem with the development of his lungs. Through prayer, and modern medicine made possible by the knowledge imparted by Our Creator, little Teaghan Mathew came home from the hospital today! I wish to thank all of those caring souls who prayed so very hard for his health. Bless you all.

Answer to Prayer:

I have been a Christian Brother for many years, but have shunned organized Orders because of a few bad apples who put personal gain or recognition before God's work. You folks seem to have introduced a breath of fresh air into the monastic life. Best Wishes this Holy Season. -Br. Thomas (Wellsville, New York)

A Song of Ascents of David.

**I was glad when they said unto me,
"Let us go into the House of the LORD."**

Our feet shall stand within your gates, Jerusalem.
Jerusalem is built as a city that is compact together;
where the tribes go up, the tribes of the LORD, as was decreed
for Israel; to give thanks to the name of the LORD.
For there are set thrones of judgment,
the thrones of the house of David.

**Pray for the peace of Jerusalem;
those who love you shall prosper.**
Peace be within your walls,
and prosperity within your palaces.
For my brethren and companion's sakes,
I will now say, "Peace be within you."
Because of the House of the Lord our God,
I will seek your good.

-Psalm 122

2.4 Charges Dismissed, Coma Ends, Benign Biopsies

"One of the Brother monks arrived in Skete,
seeking a word from Abba Moses.
The old monk answered him by saying:
'Go and sit in your cell (prayer room),
and your cell will teach
you everything.'"

-Sayings of the Desert Fathers (c. 300 A.D.)

——

"I exhort, therefore, that, first of all, supplications,
prayer, intercessions, and giving of thanks,
be made for all people."

-1 Timothy 2:1

Dec. 10, 2001 - Answer to Prayer:

Dear friends: I have emailed you on different occasions regarding my husband, Robert, an inner-city school teacher who was falsely accused of a crime. Today, praise God, the charges were dismissed. This has been a long and horrible ordeal. The charge was a felony, and would have meant the ruin of his career and time in jail. I cannot begin to express my gratitude for your prayers, and for God's mercy.

-Linda

Dec. 11, 2001 - Answer to Prayer:

I had asked for special prayer for my daughter Jennifer, and her two boys who were very sick...she called tonight and they are both well and happy, and took long naps and woke up healthy...*God answers prayer.* Thank You. Merry Christmas. Jesus is the reason for the season.

Peace, -Lynnie

48

Dec. 12, 2001 - Answer to Prayer:

Thank you so much, my daughter called and stated she feels so much better. -Joyce

---

Dec. 13, 2001 - Answer to Prayer:

My son who is 12 years old, for the past 3 years was suffering from Blood Cancer, but Jesus has healed him completely.

Thanks and regards. -Florence (Philippines)

Dec. 13, 2001 - Answer to Prayer:

I had asked for prayer for my children (5 and 7), and myself as I took my ex-wife to court, for her keeping the kids away from me. My ex-wife was found in contempt of the Court Order. The judge allowed me a little more visitation.

Thank you, and everyone who prays for these things. May God bless you, one and all. -Robert

---

Dec. 13, 2001 - Answer to Prayer:

However you give thanks, now is the time to do it. We are once again filled with hope and encouragement!!!! Steve (my nephew) is out of his coma!!! Steve is talking now... I hope my excitement is coming through here because it just is all so unbelievable. We are trying to just enjoy what we've gotten so far.

To say that Christmas has come early for our family is an understatement. Again, thank you for your continued thoughts, prayers, and concern for Steve and our family. God bless you for still being there, and for caring so much,

-Teddi (Florida)

"In worship, God imparts Himself to us."

-C.S. Lewis (1898-1963)

Dec. 13, 2001 - Answer to Prayer (Nine Days Later.)

Dear Lay Monk Preston, I sent a prayer request to you on December 4, regarding my friend and co-worker Terri. She had seven biopsies taken yesterday, and all seven came back benign today. I wholeheartedly believe this was through prayer and strong belief. She can go on to raise her 1 year-old son, and have the full and joyous life that God has meant for her.

Thank you from the bottom of my heart for all the prayers! I will certainly keep all of you in mine. -Cathy

---

Dec. 13, 2001 - Answer to Prayer:

God Bless you all for your continued support in prayer for these people and needs...I can't believe the miracles...I am healing emotionally after 15 years of abuse, and it is nothing short of miraculous. Thank You Jesus, and *Thank You!!!*

It is such a blessing to have you to stand shoulder to shoulder with, pushing back the darkness and resting in the sovereignty of Jesus...for Victory and Peace and Love...

We worship you, Lord! -Lynn

Dec. 18, 2001 - Answer to Prayer:

Praise God and all of the Prayer Warriors! Our daughter Stephanie is home, following 109 days in Seattle undergoing stem cell transplant. All is well, and I feel it is because of faith in God, and the unrelenting prayer on her behalf.

-From the bottom of our souls, *Thank All Of You,* you are truly angels. Praise the Lord!

"I saw that the most important thing I had to do was to give myself to the reading of the word, and to meditation of it."

-George Müller (1805-1898)

In the Psalms Christ Prays & Speaks About His Resurrection

A Miktam (*Golden Song*) *of David.*

Preserve me, O God. For in You, I put my trust.

I have said to the LORD: "You are My Lord;
My goodness is not needed by You,
but by the saints who are on the earth."
They are His willing ones.
In them is all My delight.

Sorrows shall be multiplied to those who run after other gods;
their drink offerings of blood I will not offer,
or even speak their names with My lips.

The LORD is the portion of My inheritance,
and of My cup. You preserve what You have given Me.
The boundary lines have fallen to Me in pleasant places.
Yes, I have a good inheritance.

I will praise the LORD, who has given me counsel.
My heart also instructs Me in the night.

I have kept My eyes always on the LORD.
Because He is at My right hand,
I shall not be overcome.
Therefore My heart is glad,
and My tongue rejoices.
My flesh also shall rest in hope.

For You will not leave My soul in Hell,
neither will You allow Your Holy One
to experience bodily corruption in the grave.

You have shown Me the path of life.
In Your presence is fullness of joy.
At Your right hand,
there are pleasures
forever.

-Psalm 16

2.5 *Prayer Warrior* Comments

I want to thank you for your Site. I was led to you by inspiration while in a state of total despair, your prayers are having an effect, and I am so grateful. I have made a strong promise to God and want to fulfill it. In addition I pray every day in the morning for all *Prayer Requests* you have online. I am not very good at it yet, but I think God gets the point.

God bless all of you, and I want to thank you for what you do. Your Brother in Christ, -Doug (Colorado)

Dear Lay Monk Preston, I can't believe that you remembered me and my prayer request from months ago!! It really touches my heart, just to know that someone I haven't even met could still remember me. Thank you. And I also want to thank you for praying for my marriage this time. I don't want to seem like I'm taking advantage, you know, continuously asking for prayer requests.

This request is very serious to me, as well as the request I had for my dad. And I would definitely love to become a *Prayer Warrior* online with this organization. I would be more than happy to pray for others. I will look on your website to see how I can join up. Again, I thank you from the bottom of my heart.

Love always, -Caroline S.

Please subscribe me to your monthly E-Newsletter. I also signed up as a *Prayer Warrior* on your *24-Hr. Prayerchain*.

-Charles E. (Mississippi)

"None can believe how powerful prayer is, and what it is able to effect, but those who have learned it by experience. It is a great matter when in extreme need to take hold on prayer."

-Martin Luther (1483-1546)

2.6 Monks On A Mission

"God had an only Son and He made him a Missionary."

-David Livingstone (1813-1873) *Africa Missionary & Explorer*

———

**"The chief danger of the Church today
is that it is trying to get on the same side as the world,**
*instead of turning the world upside down.
Our Master expects us to accomplish results,
even if they bring opposition and conflict.
Anything is better than compromise, apathy, and paralysis.
God give us an intense cry for the old-time
power of the Gospel and the Holy Spirit!"*

-A.B. Simpson (1843-1919)
Founder: *Christian & Missionary Alliance Church*

———

*"I am wired by nature to love the same toys that the world loves.
I start to fit in. I start to love what others love.
I start to call earth "home." Before you know it, I am calling
luxuries "needs" and using my money just the way unbelievers do.
I begin to forget the war. I don't think much about people perishing.
Missions and unreached people drop out of my mind.
I stop dreaming about the triumphs of grace.
I sink into a secular mind-set that looks first to what man can do,
not what God can do. It is a terrible sickness.
And I thank God for those who have forced me again and again
toward a wartime mind-set."*

**"One of the great uses of Twitter and Facebook will be to prove
at the Last Day that prayerlessness was not from lack of time."**

-John Piper (Baptist Pastor) From: *Don't Waste Your Life*

———

"You have one business on earth -- to save souls."

-John Wesley (1703-1791) Founder: *Methodists*

* * *

2.7 Dear *PrayerFoundation* ™

Thank you so much. God is so good, because when I asked to have a better prayer life, I started studying Psalms. I realized that Psalms is a prayer book and I have started praying verses and psalms I like.

Your reply must be God's way of letting me know that I am on the way to a better prayer life. Thank you for allowing God to use you to speak to me.

In Christ, -Karen W. (Virginia)

Dear *PrayerFoundation*,™ God bless you for your prayers and response. Thank you for your ministry!

Love, -Ashley D. and Family (Knoxville, Tennessee)

I am from Canada. Thanks for your prayers. I appreciate and need them. Blessings,

-Ruth S. (Canada)

Peace be with you my brothers and sisters in Christ. I am so impressed and inspired with your life together with the Most High. It is my happiness to always pray for all of you that your lives be a sweet-smelling sacrifice, acceptable to the Lord. Without people like you, I cannot imagine how the world would be.

Thank you once again, and may the peace and glory of the Lord be with you always. -Nathaniel N. (Mindanao, Philippines)

---

*"Mind how you pray. Make a real business of it.
Let it never be a dead formality...
plead the promise in a truthful, business-like way...*

Ask for what you want, because the Lord has promised it."

-Charles Spurgeon (1834-1892)

2.8 Friends of God

"'...Abraham believed God, and it was accounted to him as righteousness;' and he was called the Friend of God."

-James 2:23

"...but I have called you friends; and all things that I have heard from my Father, I have made known to you."

-John 15:15

———

"True perfection consists in having but one fear; the fear of losing God's friendship."

-St. Gregory of Nyssa (c. 335-c. 394 A.D.)

"Love Holy Scripture, and wisdom will love you. Love her, and she will keep you. Embrace her, and she will embrace you."

-St. Jerome (347-420 A.D.)

———

"Prayer is the place of refuge for every worry, a foundation for cheerfulness, a source of constant happiness, a protection against sadness."

"But first I want you to tell me this: do you know the power of love? Christ passed over all the marvelous works that were to be performed by the apostles and said, 'By this shall all know that you are my disciples, if you love one another.'"

-St. John Chrysostom (347-407 A.D.)

———

"Abba Xanthias said: 'A dog is better than I am, for he has love, and does not judge.'"

-Sayings of the Desert Fathers (c. 300 A.D.)

* * *

2.9 Lay Monk Thoughts: Humility and Love

"Humility and love, there you have it.
This is everything."

-St. Paisios of Athos (1924-1994)
Eastern Orthodox Monk

Gifts of God's Grace

The Jewish moral tradition teaches that trying to *achieve* humility is a self-defeating effort. In the New Testament, *humility* and *love* are fruit of the Holy Spirit; like salvation, they are gifts of God's grace, not attainable through human effort.

We do not have the love God wants us to have, His own love, unless it is given to us through the Holy Spirit. God's love is not something we can "work up" in and of ourselves:

"...the love of God is shed abroad in our hearts
by the Holy Spirit who is given to us." -Romans 5:5

In *practicing the presence of God* in unceasing prayer, we maintain an ever-increasing awareness of the love God gives us for others and for Him. Expressed in prayer and care for others in a life of purity and holiness; a life lived in obedience to God.

"To love God with all our hearts...
and to love our neighbors as ourselves." -Mark 12:29-31

Our Lord taught that there is no commandment greater than these This can only be accomplished *by God's grace*. It can only be accomplished *by abiding in Christ*:

"The one that abides in Me, and I in them, brings forth much fruit;
for apart from Me you can do nothing." -John 15:5

"Those that say they abide in Him,
ought also to walk, even as He walked." -1 John 2:6

* * *

56

3. *The LORD Will Provide (Yahweh Yireh)*

3.1 Obtained Facility, Cancer Gone, Atheist Saved

"Prayer breaks all bars, dissolves all chains, opens all prisons, and widens all straits by which God's saints have been held."

-E.M. Bounds (1835-1913)
Author: *Power Through Prayer*

——

"Are any among you afflicted? Let them pray. Are any happy? Let them sing psalms."

-James 5:13

Dec. 18, 2001 - Answer to Prayer:

Thank you for praying for me and my family. Rejoice! Received good news today, my hubby is a free man now!

———

Dec. 23, 2001 - Answer to Prayer:

Hi, my precious prayer family, I just want to thank you for all your loving prayer support that has carried me to Victory so many times this year. You're amazing and wonderful, and I love you so much...

I won't be spending Christmas with my family this year because of transportation problems, but I have peace and promise and *Joy;* because of your prayers and my wonderful Jesus, who is present with me to heal and comfort, and bring His peace...

Isn't *He* wonderful? -L. M.

———

*"Pray without ceasing on behalf of other men...
...for cannot he that falls rise again?"*

-St. Ignatius of Antioch
(Martyred 107/108 A.D.)

Jan. 1, 2002 - Answer to Prayer:

Last July I wrote to you about a young friend named Danny - He's doing well...He was not expected to live, it took many, many, many months...and much prayer. I thank you! I myself had never prayed so hard, I actually felt as though I did help. I know you did!

Thank You...and I remember you in prayer also. -Michele

(*Note* from the *PrayerFoundation:*™ Thank you so much. Your remembering us in prayer is the kind of support we most desire, and for which we are most thankful.)

Jan. 2, 2002 - Prayer Request:

I am self-employed and I had a project scheduled at a facility...I got a call tonight and they said that the space will not be available to me as promised. This is devastating, because the contract with my client is based on our using that facility.

I can't afford a more expensive one; plus, I have already been paid and have used a lot of the money, thinking the promise from a major university was sound.

Please pray that we will be able to get this space on the date and at the cost promised. Thank you and God bless, -Jane (Virginia)

Answer to Prayer – Jan. 11, 2002 (Nine Days Later.)

Praise the Lord!! We got the facility on Feb. 18th as promised. Thank you for praying, -Jane (Virginia)

Jan. 8, 2002 - Answer to Prayer:

Those prayers surely did work, I went to the Dr. today and got my MRI'S and CAT scans.

I Am Cancer Free -- The Prayers Worked -- Thank You, Thank You All So Much!

With Christian Love, -Yvonne

Jan. 8, 2002 - Answer to Prayer:

Over the past year, I asked for prayer regarding my relationship with my brother-in-law Gary. I would like to tell you that those prayers *did* make a difference!

A year ago, we would just say hello at family functions...this after five years of knowing each other. Today, not only do we socialize more, but we have become each other's best friend.

Certain situations have confirmed that I heard *God* correctly in my spirit...that I was to ask for prayer to make this relationship blossom. So again, I would like to thank you for your prayers over the past year regarding this request. God did hear them.

I give this report as encouragement, and so that we all may give the Lord Jesus the praise He so rightly deserves. He truly cares about the details in our lives...and I have seen that the Lord also reveals Himself to us, through the love and service of others (inspired by the Holy Spirit).

So, praise the Lord with me, because He is so worthy of our praise and service. Praise and exalt His Name and Being, above all that has been created and is in existence. He is so worthy of our love, adoration, and service; now and for all eternity. Jesus is Lord!

With lots of love in Christ Jesus, -Rob L.

Jan. 9, 2002 - Answer to Prayer:

I wish to let you know, that my friend has been told the bone marrow transplant is working thus far, and the Cancer is gone; however, there is still a long road ahead, and much prayer is still needed for his total recovery.

Thank You, -J.M.

"Nothing that is God's is obtainable by money."

-Tertullian (c.155-c. 220 A.D.)

Jan. 9, 2002 - Answer to Prayer:

A Praise Report for God bringing my brother, a self-proclaimed atheist, back to Him; so that my brother now is praising God and Jesus, praying, and repenting; *Praise God!!!*

Thank you and God Bless you, and all of your loved ones. -Jason

---

Jan. 10, 2002 - Answer to Prayer:

A while back, I asked if you all could pray for my mom; her husband just died in November of 2002, and I asked if you all could pray for her to have amazing strength. Well, she has amazing strength, and that's because of all the prayers you prayed; so thank you for reading my email, and praying for my mom and my sister.

Happy New Year, -Sandy A.

A Song of Ascents.

If it had not been the LORD who was on our side,
now may Israel say:

"If it had not been the LORD who was on our side,
when people rose up against us;
then they had swallowed us up quick,
when their wrath was kindled against us;
then the waters had overwhelmed us,
the stream had gone over our soul;
then the proud waters had gone over our soul.

Praised be the LORD,
who has not given us as prey to their teeth.
Our soul has escaped like a bird
out of the net of the hunters.
The net has broken, and we have escaped.

**Our help is in the name of the LORD,
who made heaven and earth."**

-Psalm 124

3.2 Moslem Father Saved, No More Chemo, Leukemia Gone

"It is not enough to begin to pray, nor to pray aright;
nor is it enough to continue for a time to pray;
but we must pray patiently, believing,
continue in prayer until we obtain an answer."

-George Müller (1805-1898)

———

"And He told a parable to them to this end,
that one ought always to pray, and not to give up."

-Luke 18:1

Feb. 13, 2002 - Answer to Prayer:

My daughter is getting better and better every day. Thank you all so much for your prayers, and please don't stop lifting her up, until she is completely healed of all her medical problems.

Thank you and God Bless you all. -Brother Aldo (Italy)

———

Feb. 14, 2002 - Answer to Prayer:

Greetings, *PrayerFoundation*:™ A while back, I sent in a prayer request for my friend, and for my step-mother. I just wanted to share with you that my friend is doing much better and continues to hold his own and improve. My step-mother is doing fine. She still has other treatments to undergo, but so far things seem to be coming along well. I thank everyone for their prayers. God truly answers prayer. Thank You and God Bless.

———

"Ho, every one that thirsts, come to the waters;
and he that has no money: come, buy, and eat.
Yes, come buy wine and milk, without money and without price."

-Isaiah 55:1

Feb. 17, 2002 - Answer to Prayer:

...thank God for the provisions of Internet fellowships and *You:* friendships, the gift of prayer, and the forgiveness, mercy, grace, and the undying love of the Lord Jesus Christ. Thank you from deep within my heart for all your warm thoughts, encouragement, and prayers given toward me throughout this time, also.

Truly, -Patti

Feb. 20, 2002 - Answer to Prayer:

Dear in Christ, Praise be to the Lord!

My father died just two months ago. He was 90 years of age and a retired Headmaster / Principal. He was a staunch Muslim, President of the Jama'ath Committee (*Muslim Diocesan Committee*) for a long time and was very particular in the rituals of Islam.

But a few months before his death he fully heard about Jesus from me and accepted Him as his personal Saviour. -Ciniraj (India)

Feb. 25, 2002 - Answer to Prayer:

Just want to send you an update about Nicco, and thank you so much for praying for him. Nicco turned 5 on February 4th, and he is doing well. Wednesday, February 20th, the hospital had an off-Chemo party for him with a lot of people attending. It was a very happy occasion.

The last MRI still does not show any more shrinkage of the tumor, but the Doctors look at how well he is doing, and they are very optimistic about his future. They say they cannot explain why the tumor stopped growing, but we tell them it is because of all the prayers that have been said for him.

Nicco is catching up fast, he is speaking quite well, and his strength is coming back. He has also started preschool, and he loves it.

By the way, Nicco had an IQ test, and after all he has gone through, he tested above normal. He truly is a miracle.

S.G. Preston

The last 2 years have not been easy, and I know that it is your prayers that have pulled us through. Thank you and may God bless you. Love, -Thordis (Nicco's Grandma)

Answer to Prayer Update - June 10, 2002

Again, thank you to all of you who are praying for Nicco, and have sent us letters of concern and encouragement. On Tuesday, Nicco had another MRI of the brainstem tumor, and the results are good...the MRI clearly shows that the tumor has dead pockets inside. His fighting spirit is so strong in him, and we know it has become stronger because of your prayers. Thank you so much to all of you...

God bless you all. -Thordis and Ellen

Feb. 28, 2002 - Prayer Request:

Dear friends, prayer request for our Worship Leader, Jim. Jim was found to have leukemia last week and admitted to hospital. He just finished his first round of Chemo. This week his body has to rejuvenate and remake the good blood cells he needs. On Monday he'll be tested to see if this is happening.

Pray that Jesus heals him. Also uphold Jim's wife and children: Wendy and Jamie, praying *the peace that passeth all understanding* into their hearts.

Another request is that God provide financially. Jim's Insurance will only cover this hospital stay. I am hoping that the healing touch of our Lord would indeed be poured into Jim's body, in such a way that he would require no more hospitalization. I want to thank you for praying for Jim.

God Bless You. Love, -Mo

Answer to Prayer - Mar. 6, 2002 (6 Days Later)

I am just sending you an update on Jim who has Leukemia. It is a wonderful praise. Today the results of the bone marrow came back and it is cancer free. It is wonderful news.

Once again, I can only say thank you, and that Jim and Kim would thank you personally themselves if they could. We so appreciate all of your prayers.

Love, -Mo

P.S. ...there is a wonderful Christian man who is willing to pay all financial outlays of Kim and Jim's over this time, so that when they return home there will be no debt at all. Again this is just God's abundant provision. I have tears in my eyes typing this, as I feel very blessed to see God's hand outworking all of this.

Thank you once again.

A Song of Ascents.

Those that trust in the LORD shall be like Mount Zion, which cannot be removed, but remains forever.
As the mountains surround Jerusalem,
so the LORD surrounds His people;
from this time forward, forever and ever.

For the rod of the wicked shall not rest on the lot of the godly;
so that the godly do not put forth their hands to wickedness.

Do good, O LORD, to those that are good,
and to those that are upright in their hearts.

As for those that turn aside to their crooked ways,
the LORD shall lead them forth with those who do evil;
but peace shall rest upon Israel.

-Psalm 125

———

*"Every great movement of God
can be traced to a kneeling figure."*

*"Next to the wonder of seeing my Savior will be, I think,
the wonder that I made so little use of the power of prayer."*

-Dwight Moody (1837-1899) World Evangelist

3.3 Charges Dropped, Have Rent Money, Still Leukemia Free

*"Not to pray because you
do not feel like praying
is like saying,
'I will not take my medicine
because I am too ill.'"*

-Charles Spurgeon (1834-1892)
Author: *The Treasury of David*
(Commentary on the Psalms)

———

*"Are any sick among you?
Let them call for the
Elders of the church;
and let the Elders
pray over them,
anointing them with oil
in the name of the Lord.
And the prayer of faith
will save the sick person,
and the Lord will raise them up;
and if they have committed sins,
they shall be forgiven."*

-James 5:14-15

Mar. 3, 2002 - Answer to Prayer:

Greetings, I have submitted two prayer requests; one for a friend with Cancer who underwent a bone marrow transplant, and one for my step-mother who was facing eye surgery.

God has blessed them with his healing, and the prayers were answered. My friend continues to improve and my step mother is slowly recovering. Thank you so much for your prayers.

Mar. 5, 2002 - Answer to Prayer:

Thank you for all your prayers. Today I received a miracle…the D.A. decided to drop the charge against me. I do believe in the power of prayer and miracles.

All I ever asked, was that the *Truth* be known, and today after three long years, I got my answer...a dismissal of a crime that I never did commit. Thank you everyone for praying for me. I am forever in your debt.

Love, -Susan

Mar. 7, 2002 - Answer to Prayer:

Thank you all for praying. Two weeks ago you prayed for me to be able to pay my rent, and on March 2nd I got enough money to add to what I earned at my retail job, to pay rent.

I was short about $200.00, when a man I know needed help at a trade show. So for 2 days I answered questions at his booth and on the 2nd day he paid me. I had $75 left over. Then I won a contest at my job that gave me another $40.

-God is faithful.

Mar. 11, 2002 - Answer to Prayer:

Jerrad made it through the critical 24 hours, thanks to all your prayers. -E.M.J.

"Prayer does not mean simply to pour out one's heart.

It means rather to find the way to God
and to speak with Him,
whether the heart is full or empty.

No man can do that by himself.
For that he needs Jesus Christ."

-Dietrich Bonhoeffer (1906-1945)

66

Mar. 20, 2002 - Answer to Prayer:

Jesus always Triumphs (2 Corinthians 2:14). I wish I could put into words what your prayer ministry has meant to me. Because of the love of Jesus, and the prayers of your ministering saints, I am out of an abusive relationship. I have been carried financially after a long siege of financial drought, been emotionally healed after 12 years of abuse, been given the gift of a Christian man and a 12 year old boy who are like family and are my future and my hope, been healed so quickly from a car accident that no one can believe it, and so much more... How can I say Thanks...

I *Know* God gets all the glory, and I am in awe of His mercy and presence, even when I was too tired to pray. But I also *Know* our Father wants us to *Feel* the *Joy* He gets when we unite and hold each other up, and help walk them through to Victory and Promise, and that is what you have done, and I am forever grateful.

Praise be to God for *You*...My wonderful prayer family. I love you with the precious love of Jesus + -L.

Mar. 20, 2002 - Answer to Prayer:

Dear Friends, I wrote you some days ago for Claire, my sister-in-law, and one of my requests has been answered: I said I didn't know how to act anymore, and since I've seen her again, the "ideas" keep coming back. Though others tell me not to intervene because I'm "only" her in-law, I know that if God shows me *something* I can do for her, even the tiniest thing, I mustn't miss it, no matter what may happen.

I was even very less scared the day I went to see her (Tuesday). I felt so many people thinking and praying for us, and when she heard me say, "Hello, sweetie!" she gave me a ray of sunshine. She smiled from one ear to the other; it was the most wonderful present she could give me, and the sign that I must follow my heart; that this means following God. Thank you!

God Bless You All, -Ariane (Belgium)

Mar. 4, 2002 - Prayer Request:

Please pray for our son-in-law, Eric; age 54. He had surgery on his forearm for a Melanoma Cancer about 6 weeks ago. On March 21st, they took two lymph nodes from his armpit. We are waiting for the pathology report this week. Please pray the Lord has and will, prevent any cancer cells from spreading.

He is a Baptist minister and loves the ministry and his people. We are asking Jesus to give him many more years of fruitful ministry. He pastors in Ontario, Canada.

Thank you so much for your prayers. -Etta (Ohio)

Answer to Prayer - Mar. 6, 2002 (Two Days Later.)

Dear friends in Christ, The pathology report on Eric's lymph nodes is benign. Thank you so much.

Your sister in Christ, -Etta (Ohio)

Answer to Prayer Update - June 9, 2002

Dear Lay Monks, I wanted to once again thank you for praying for Jim, who had leukemia. I have not posted any updates because he has been doing really well. Kim did send me the first update in a month and it is all good news.

Jim has one round of Chemo left, and I wanted to let you know that each time he has undergone Chemo and the doctors have tested his blood, he is Cancer free.

-Thank you once again for all of your prayers.

"This, I say, is the end of all perfection,
that the mind purged from all carnal desires
may daily be lifted toward spiritual things,
until the whole life and all thoughts of the heart
become one continuous prayer."

-St. John Cassian (360-435 A.D.) Monk

68

A Song of Ascents.

When the LORD returned us from captivity back to Zion, we were like those that dream.

Then our mouth was filled with laughter,
and our tongue with singing.

Then they said among the nations,
"The LORD has done great things for them."

The LORD has done great things for us; we are joyful.

Renew our fortunes, O LORD,
like you renew the streams in the desert.

Those who sow in tears, shall reap in joy.

Those who go out weeping,
bearing precious seed,
shall certainly return rejoicing,
bringing in their harvest.

-Psalm 126

———

*"The work of praying is prerequisite
to all other work in the kingdom of God,
for the simple reason that it is by prayer
that we couple the powers of heaven
to our helplessness,*

*the powers which can turn water into wine
and remove mountains in our own life
and in the lives of others,
the powers which can awaken
those who sleep in sin and raise up the dead,*

*the powers which can capture strongholds
and make the impossible possible."*

-O. Hallesby (1879-1961) Author of the book: *Prayer*
Norwegian Lutheran Pastor; Imprisoned Two Years in a
Concentration Camp for Opposition to the Nazis

3.4 Biopsy Benign, Grant Received, Chemo Not Needed

"There is not in the world
a kind of life
more sweet and delightful,
than that of a
continual conversation
with God;

those only can comprehend it,
who practice and
experience it."

-Brother Lawrence (c. 1614-1691)
From: *The Practice of the Presence of God*

———

"Taste and see that the LORD is good;
blessed are those who
take refuge in Him."

-Psalm 34:8

Apr. 30, 2002 - Prayer Request:

Please pray for my mother, Helen. She is very ill. She is 58 years old, and a biopsy of her lungs and liver has been scheduled for Wednesday.

Pray that she has a healing, in Jesus' name. -Marian

Answer to Prayer - May 1, 2002 (One Day Later.)

Thank you for praying for my mother, Helen. She had a scheduled biopsy on Wednesday. They performed an ultrasound before the biopsy and found nothing serious enough to justify a biopsy on her liver and lungs. Miraculous healing!!!!!

Praise the Lord!!! Alleluia!!! -Marian

May 14, 2002 - Answer to Prayer:

I am an artist/businessperson who has waited ten years to receive the blessing that has befallen me recently. I have been granted monies to complete my work. *Thank God!* Thanking God also for the blessings it will bring, and I am thankful today for independence being restored, inner peace, true friends, quality relationships, and true love - also wisdom and divine guidance in Christ. Thank you!!!

-Lee (New York City)

May 28, 2002 - Answer to Prayer:

Stephanie continues slow, steady progress, 9 months post-transplant; all indicators are positive, thank you all for continued prayers for her. Still far from full recovery, but we thank God she is doing so well, each day has a new meaning for our family now.

God bless you all. -Kevin

June 7, 2002 - Answer to Prayer:

Praise the Lord!!! He worked a miracle! My sister-in-law Ruthie's surgery was successful. Her Pancreatic Cancer hadn't spread, and she won't even need Chemo or Radiation. Thank you for interceding on her behalf; your thoughts and prayers are gratefully appreciated.

God bless you. God is good! -Ginny

"It can happen that when we are at prayer
some brothers come to see us.
Then we have to choose either to interrupt our prayer
or to sadden our brother by refusing to answer him.

But love is greater than prayer.
Prayer is one virtue among others,
whereas love contains them all."

-St. John Climacus (c. 579-649 A.D.) Monk

3.5 *Prayer Warrior* Comments

I have been a daily visitor to your website for about 3 months. It is a tremendous encouragement. I am in the U.K. and am able to pray Sunday mornings from 6 a.m. for a minimum of 15 minutes - usually more.

Apart from the commitment to pray made to the *Prayerchain, PrayerFoundation's* ™ ministry is on my prayer list.

Yours in His service, -Brother Bruce (England)

(Survey) *Visit Site:* **Daily.** *Comments:* **I've been praying for the prayer requests** for a while now, and I know it's a privilege to do so. I've recently signed up for your E-Newsletter... Your ministry has changed my life. Thank you!

With love in Jesus, -Kathie (California)

Dear Brothers of the *PrayerFoundation.*™ I would like to enlist in the group of your *24-Hr. Prayerchain.* I have seen so much pain in this world, and we all need the help of others to able to cope with the many tribulations that sometimes come our way.

We need the support of others, and also our obligation is to console the sick and the needy, and the lonely of heart and soul. There are countless people at this terrible time unemployed; there are at this time countless people frightened; scared of the unknown enemy.

But with the help of each other, and Faith in the Help of God we must prevail as children of the Highest. -R.M. (Nevada)

---

*"God did not tell us to follow Him
because He needed our help,
but because He knew that loving Him
would make us whole."*

-St. Irenaeus of Lyons
(c. 120/140-c. 200/203 A.D.)

3.6 The Cost of Discipleship

*"Prayer means not always talking to Him,
but (also) waiting before Him
till the dust settles and the stream runs clear."*

*"We must alter our lives in order to alter our hearts,
for it is impossible to live one way and pray another."*

*"They, therefore, who are hasty in their devotions
and think a little will do, are strangers both to
the nature of devotion and the nature of man;
they do not know that they are to learn to pray,
and that prayer is to be learned as they learn other things,
by frequency, constancy, and perseverance."*

*"Fall on your knees and grow there.
There is no burden of the spirit
but is lighter by kneeling under it."*

-William Law (1686-1761) Anglican Priest
Lost his position at Cambridge for refusing to
take an oath of allegiance to King George I

———

*"Prayer is the supreme instance of the hidden character
of the Christian life."*

*"Intercessory prayer is the purifying bath into which the community
and the individual must enter every day."*

**"It matters little what form of prayer we adopt or how many words
we use. What matters is the faith which lays hold on God,
knowing that He knows our needs before we even ask Him.
That is what gives Christian prayer its boundless confidence
and its buoyant certainty."**

-Dietrich Bonhoeffer (1906-1945) Lutheran Theologian
Imprisoned and Martyred by the Nazis for opposing Hitler
Author: *Psalms: The Prayer Book of the Bible*
and *The Cost of Discipleship*

* * *

3.7 Dear *PrayerFoundation* ™

I thank you again for your loving prayers for Lisa and I, for our marriage, for our ministry, for us. They have meant so much, and they mean more now than they ever have. Thank you!

In the midst of this great struggle I am finding God's peace and strength. Thank you again, and God bless! Agape', -Brice W.

God bless you.

-Max and Sheila (Hokkaido, Japan)

The needs of people mostly come to the fore during times of prayer. Your friend,

-Pastor Johan L.; *Missionary* (Nelspruit, South Africa)

Just wanted to let you know that praying *The Threefold Daily Prayers* has been a real blessing in my life.

Bless you all and keep up the great work. -Bray (Texas)

Thank you for the ways you are allowing God to use you to benefit others...

-Lay Monk Justin (Vienna, Austria)

Good afternoon, is your DVD *Peter and Paul* also with the possibility of Dutch sub-titling...? Best regards,

-Jos. S.; *Master Catechetics, Diocese of Rotterdam* (Netherlands)

"Seek the truth, listen to the truth,
teach the truth, love the truth, abide by the truth,
and defend the truth unto death."

-Jan Hus (c.1372-1415)
Martyr: burned at the stake.

74

I am a pastor (Presbyterian). I appreciate your website and its wonderful information. -Dr. Eugene B. (South Carolina)

First of all, I would like to thank you for what you are doing, it is a great blessing. I am very eager to become a Lay Monk. I am a Theology Major with an emphasis in Biblical Studies at Colorado Christian University and am constantly studying the Bible. This Semester I have to read the entire Bible just to pass my courses. Also, I have to complete readings on Biblical Commentaries and Exegesis and Hermeneutics.

...I want to follow your Course as truly as possible. Blessings in Him, -Benjamin L. (Denver, Colorado)

Thanks for all of you wonderful *Prayer Warriors!* You sure give hope and strength to people like me, who feel alone at times.

Thanks for the prayers. They work! -T.J.

I wanted to tell you that after I requested prayer last week, I felt a change in my mental outlook and a real peace about my circumstances. I feel more optimistic about my future and my faith in God is stronger. I believe God healed me emotionally.

-Marquita (Seattle, Washington)

Thank you for your kindness and for your prayers and also for you being a blessing to me during this time. I do not know what might have happened to me if I had not followed that still small voice a few months ago when it told me to ask for prayer for myself and also prayer for my children. I have felt the spirit of God in life the last few months and I have had things happen in my life that I did not think would happen.

The most important event during this time has been that God has placed a number of wonderful people of God in my life. I praise him for letting me meet you over the Internet and if it is not meant for us to ever meet in this world then I am assured that I will meet you when we all go home to be with our Father.

I know without a doubt that our Father is going to bless you because of the work that you're doing for Him.

Love In Jesus' name, -Margie

I have requested prayer from your organization before and always have had fast and great rewards...my kids are all fine, thanks to God. My 95 yr. old mom is also ok. I am grateful and give thanks for all the positives in my life.

Thank you for all your prayers. As this week unfolds, I go with a wonderful feeling in my heart that all my prayers will be answered because of your help. Thank you and Happy Holidays.

God bless you all! -Claire (Texas)

A friend of mine at **** would probably be interested in your group.** Thank you for your prayers, many have been answered! -(Request to send me your E-Newsletter.)

I think you are doing wonderful work - your prayers have helped me - I am certain. Thank you for the good work you do. -Kim L.

Thank you so much for your continued prayer. It is a great comfort. I thank you, and thank the Lord for your website. -Tom B.

Dear Brothers, I am very glad that you took my needs seriously (that's current English?) and are praying to the Lord Jesus therefore! Thank you very much! Blessings! -Uli (Germany)

"Christ desires His mysteries to be published abroad as widely as possible. I would that (the Gospels and the Epistles of Paul) were translated into all languages... and that they might be read and known."

-William Tyndale (c. 1490-1536)
Martyred for Translating the Bible into English

A Song of Ascents of Solomon.

**Unless the LORD builds the house,
its builders labor without success.**

Unless the LORD protects the city,
its watchmen stay awake in vain.

It is foolish for you to rise up early and stay up late,
toiling just to eat the bread of sorrows;
for He gives His beloved sleep.

Children are a gift from the LORD;
the fruit of the womb is a reward.

Like arrows in the hand of a mighty man,
even so are the children of your youth.
Happy are those that have a quiver full of them!

They shall not be put to shame
when they contend against their enemies,
in the courts held at the city gate.

-Psalm 127

———

A Song of Ascents.

**Blessed are all those who reverence the LORD;
who walk in His ways.**

For you shall eat the labor of your hands.
You shall be happy, and it shall be well with you.

Your wife shall be like a fruitful vine by the side of your house;
your children like olive shoots around your table.

**See how the man who reverences the LORD is blessed!
The LORD shall bless you from Zion,**
and you shall see the prosperity of Jerusalem
all the days of your life.
Yes, you shall see your children's children,
and peace in Israel.

-Psalm 128

3.8 E.M. Bounds (1835-1913) On Prayer

"God shapes the world by prayer.

The prayers of God's saints are the capital stock of heaven by which God carries on His great work upon the earth."

"Prayer is God's plan to supply man's great and continuous need with God's great and continuous abundance."

——

"No Insistence in the Scripture is more pressing than that we must pray...

How clear it is, when the Bible is consulted, that the Almighty God is brought directly into the things of this world by the prayers of His people."

"We cannot talk to God strongly when we have not lived for God strongly.

The prayer room cannot be made holy to God when the life has not been holy to God."

——

"Prayer is far-reaching in its influence and worldwide in its effects. It affects all men, affects them everywhere, and affects them in all things.

It touches man's interest in time and eternity.

It lays hold upon God and moves Him to intervene in the affairs of earth.

It moves the angels to minister to men in this life.

It restrains and defeats the devil in his schemes to ruin man.

Prayer goes everywhere and lays its hand on everything."

——

"Prayer is our most formidable weapon, the thing that makes all else we do efficient."

——

*"Whatever affects the intensity of our praying
affects the intensity of our work."*

———

"True prayers are born of present trials and present needs.

*Bread for today is bread enough.
Bread given for today is the strongest sort of pledge
that there will be bread tomorrow.
Victory today is the assurance of victory tomorrow.*

*Our prayers need to be focused on the present.
We must trust God today,
and leave the morrow entirely with Him.
The present is ours; the future belongs to God.*

*Prayer is the task and duty of each recurring day
-- daily prayer for daily needs."*

———

*"Pray for 'all men.'
We usually pray more for things than we do for men.*

*Our prayers should be thrown across their pathway
as they rush in their downward course to a long eternity."*

———

**"'Be careful for nothing, but in everything,
by supplication and prayer, with thanksgiving,
let your requests be made known unto God.'**

*That is the Divine cure for all fear,
anxiety, and undue concern of soul,
all of which are closely akin
to doubt and unbelief."*

———

**"The ministry of prayer, if it be anything worthy of the name,
is a ministry of unwearied and intense longing
after God and after His holiness."**

* * *

3.9 Lay Monk Thoughts: Purity & Holiness

"As He who has called you is holy, so be holy in all manner of lifestyle; because it is written: 'Be holy, for I am holy.'"

-1 Peter 1:15-16

———

"Do you not know that you are God's temple, and that the Spirit of God dwells in you?"

-1 Corinthians 3:16

Enter Through the Narrow Gate

...For wide is the gate leading to destruction (Matthew 7:13). The world offers a seemingly infinite number of ways to waste our lives and destroy our souls. The gateway to life is as narrow as a needle's eye: it is Christ Himself.

In the Greek of the New Testament, the word for sin is *hamartia* (ἀμαρτία - *missing the mark*). It is a reference to shooting an arrow at a target. You either *hit the bullseye,* or you don't.

When Jesus was going to wash Peter's feet (John 13:1-17), Peter refused, and Jesus told him that if he didn't wash Peter's feet, Peter could have no part in Jesus. Peter said, *"Then wash my hands and head also."* Jesus answered that one who is clean need only have his feet washed.

We who have received Christ have been cleansed of sin, but walking through this world our feet get dirty with sins, and we need forgiveness. Jesus said we are to wash others feet (forgive them) as He washes our feet (forgives us).

Cleansed in body, our feet washed daily by Christ, we can go forth into the world as Christ's ambassadors. Jesus said, *"I have set you an example that you should do as I have done for you."*

"...set the believers an example in speech, in conduct, in love, in faith, in purity."

-1 Timothy 4:12

* * *

80

4. *The LORD is There* (*Yahweh Shammah*)

4.1 Gospel in Portland, Africa Graduation, Coughing Healed

"Only a life of prayer and meditation
will render a vessel fit
for the Master's use."

-George Müller (1805-1898)

———

"Confess your faults one to another,
and pray for one another,
that you may be healed."

-James 5:16

May 6, 2002 - Urgent Prayer Request:

Please pray that Title 14 of the City Code in Portland, Oregon *not* be changed. There is an attempt to change Title 14, so that Street Preachers can be stopped from sharing the Gospel, by punishing them with a $1,000 fine, and six months in jail.

Because the city cannot legally block freedom of speech, they are trying to pass a new ordinance that they can selectively enforce at will against anyone who is not continuously moving (is pausing) in a public area.

This includes such things as sitting on a public bench. Anyone preaching would be considered to be "blocking public access" to that bench's use (or any public area).

Also, authority for enforcement would be extended beyond the Police, to private security guards. This would mean that any private business owner (with a security guard) who doesn't like the Gospel, could have Christians fined $1,000.00 and jailed for six months.

-Lay Monk Bob (Portland, Oregon)

Answer to Prayer - July 22, 2002

It was defeated!!! Praise the Lord for answering prayer! And we thank you all for praying!

-Lay Monk Bob (Portland, Oregon)

May 17, 2003 - Prayer Request:

Friends, I am under attack; I was supposed to graduate this coming Friday. Now I'm told that I failed; yet in February I was told that I had passed, and was asked to do an honors degree, but I declined. Please pray with me, I am believing God for a miracle. By faith I will be graduating; to the glory of God the Father, in Jesus' Name, Amen.

No weapon formed against us shall prosper; and if Christ be for us, who can be against us" -K. (Swaziland)

Answer to Prayer - May 19, 2003 (Two Days Later.)

Praise God, my request has been granted. It's official, as of 1043 Hrs. today, that I will be graduating over the weekend.

May God richly bless you, and continue to further His Kingdom through you, brethren. Amen. -K. (Swaziland)

June 11, 2002 - Urgent Prayer Request:

Please pray for my Mom, age 70, who is having a hysterectomy surgery on Friday; that everything would go well with it.
-(Wisconsin)

Answer to Prayer - June 14, 2002 (Three Days Later.)

Praise God! My Mom's surgery went well, and the polyp that was found and removed was not Cancerous! -(Wisconsin)

---

*"Unless we fix certain hours in the day for prayer,
it easily slips our memory."*

-John Calvin (1509-1564)

June 11, 2002 - Urgent Prayer Request:

I am very sick, with non-stop coughing (cold/flu/pneumonia related), please pray for a complete healing for me. -(Oregon)

Answer to Prayer - June 15, 2002 (Four Days Later.)

The Lord has answered the prayers, and healed the terrible non-stop coughing and fever that I had. -(Oregon)

June 15, 2002 - Answer to Prayer:

I want to say that things always go so well for us when I send in a prayer request; maybe not immediately, but real soon thereafter. I am having to relocate all my family to Houston for a better paying job; to afford my mom going to assisted living, or for a private duty nurse at home.

My cousin has stepped in and leased me her house in a very nice area. I already found a job; I start June 26th. It's all going well. The good news is, my husband has passed his certification courses and has been offered a job in Houston upon his release in Nov. 2003.

Isn't that great! God is Good!! Thank you so much for all of your past efforts, they have really made a difference. I'll keep in touch. Much love from all of us, to all of you!!

R., C., J.M., B., T., C., G.K. (Houston, Texas)

"Sometimes when we read the words of those who have been more than conquerors, we feel almost despondent. I feel that I shall never be like that. But they won through step by step, by little bits of wills, little denials of self, little inward victories, by faithfulness in very little things. They became what they are."

"If you are ever inclined to pray for a missionary, do it at once, wherever you are. Perhaps they may be in great peril at that moment."

-Amy Carmichael (1867-1951) Irish Missionary to India
Founder: *Dohnavur Fellowship Orphanage*

4.2 Son Off Heroin, Gospel in China, God Provides for Baby

*"I would rather teach one man to pray
than ten men to preach."*

-Charles Spurgeon (1834-1892)
Author: *The Treasury of David*
(Commentary on the Psalms)

———

*"But my God shall supply all your needs,
according to His riches in glory
by Christ Jesus."*

-Philippians 4:19

June 17, 2002 - Answer to Prayer:

I had requested prayer for my financial situation and for my son who had a drug problem, and also is facing a trial for burglaries. My financial situation is *much* improved. Thank you so much for your prayers. I thought the only solution would be to win the lottery or something. However, God had other plans.

My husband had been paying a huge amount of support to his ex-wife. She took him to Court for more. The Judge decided in his favor, and he doesn't have to pay any anymore. This is incredible and certainly an answer to prayers. Now we have enough money to pay the bills! Also, my son is doing well, and is now off drugs.

Thank you so very much for your prayers. -Mom in Pennsylvania

Answer to Prayer Update - Aug. 8, 2002

You have been praying for my son. He was addicted to heroin, lost his house and good job, and was falsely accused by his girlfriend (when she was caught) of house robberies that she had committed. He is now working hard, and has not used drugs for six months.

Thank you so much, -Mom in Pennsylvania

S.G. Preston

July 26, 2002 - Answer to Prayer:

I am so thankful for your prayers. I am now Cancer free. You helped guide me when I needed it the most.

Thanks. -Yvonne (Baton Rouge, Louisiana)

Sept. 14, 2002 - Answer To Prayer

My name is Joyce, and I sent you all several prayer requests for my daughter. She is doing so much better. I plan to move her out here in November. Health-wise, God has truly blessed us.

Thank you all for your prayers. Thank you, thank you, thank you, and Praise the Lord!!!

Thank you all so much!!! -Joyce

Oct. 14, 2002 - Urgent Prayer Request:

Dear *Prayer Warriors*, Please pray for a young woman who is pregnant and is unmarried.

Please pray for both her health, and her unborn baby's health; that God would provide all her and her baby's needs, and provide the emotional support that she needs.

Thank you, -J. (New Zealand)

Answer to Prayer - Oct. 15, 2002 (One Day Later.)

Dear *Prayer Warriors*, praise God, that the single pregnant woman that I requested prayer for, is doing very well physically and emotionally. She has seen some very unexpected provision from God, of things that she needed for her baby.

God is answering, and through His generous provision, is encouraging this mum-to-be; about His concern and love for both her, and her unborn baby. Thank you for your prayers, and may God continue to bless your ministry and you all personally, in your areas of need.

-J. (New Zealand)

Answer to Prayer Update - Oct. 27, 2002

Dear *Prayer Warriors*, God is continuing to answer my prayer request of 14th October for the single pregnant woman. Her pregnancy continues to go well, and she is emotionally in very good spirits amidst difficult circumstances. She continues to see God's provision, for the needs of herself and her unborn baby.

Thank you. -J. (New Zealand)

Answer to Prayer Update - Feb. 4, 2003 (8 Months Later.)

Dear *Prayer Warriors*, praise God that the young pregnant woman that I requested prayer for last year had tests that came back surprising; indicating that her baby is in the very low risk group of major chromosomal abnormalities. The scan results have been good, with just one more to go in just over two weeks, to check the baby's heart arteries. The baby is exactly on target in growth.

-J. (New Zealand)

The LORD is righteous, loosing the wicked, so Christ's shed blood would bring Salvation: *"...with His stripes we are healed."* (Isaiah 53:5)

A Song of Ascents.

Many a time they have afflicted me from my youth,
may Israel now say: Many a time they have afflicted me from my
youth, yet they have not prevailed against me.
The plowers plowed upon my back;
they made their furrows long.
The LORD is righteous. He has cut apart the ropes of the wicked.

Let all those who hate Zion be
thrown into confusion and turned back.
Let them be like the grass on the housetops,
which withers before it has fully grown.
The one who harvests it cannot fill his hands with it,
or the one who would bind it together in bundles.
Those that go by will not say to them, "The blessing of the LORD
be with You; we bless you in the name of the LORD."
-Psalm 129

S.G. Preston

**"Who has believed our report?
And to who is the arm of the LORD revealed?**
For He shall grow up before Him as a tender plant, and as a root out
of dry ground; He has no form or comeliness, and when we shall see
Him, there is no beauty that we should desire Him.
**He is despised and rejected of men; a man of sorrows,
and acquainted with grief; and we hid our faces from Him;
He was despised, and we esteemed Him not.**
Surely, He has borne our griefs, and carried our sorrows:
yet we did esteem Him stricken, smitten of God, and afflicted.
**But He was wounded for our transgressions, He was bruised for
our iniquities; the chastisement of our peace was upon Him;
and with His stripes we are healed.
All we like sheep have gone astray;
we have turned every one to His own way;
and the LORD has laid on Him the iniquity of us all.**
He was oppressed, and He was afflicted, yet He opened not His
mouth; He was brought as a lamb to the slaughter, and as a sheep
before its shearers is silent, so He opened not His mouth.
He was taken from prison and from judgment; and who shall declare
His generation? He was cut off out of the land of the living;
for the transgression of my people He was stricken.
**And He made His grave with the wicked,
and with the rich in His death; because He had done no violence,
neither was any deceit in His mouth**.
Yet it pleased the LORD to bruise Him; He has put Him to grief.
When You shall make His soul an offering for sin, He shall see His
offspring; He shall prolong His days, and the pleasure of the LORD
shall prosper in His hand.
**He shall see the travail of His soul, and shall be satisfied;
by His knowledge my Righteous Servant shall justify many;
for He shall bear their iniquities.**
Therefore I will divide Him a portion with the great, and He shall
divide the spoil with the strong; because He has poured out His soul
to death; and He was numbered with the transgressors; and He bore
the sin of many, and made intercession for the transgressors."

-Isaiah 53

87

4.3 D.C. Snipers Caught, Can Now Have Baby, Depression Gone

"Talking to men for God is a great thing,
but talking to God for men
is greater still."

-E.M. Bounds (1835-1913)
Author: *Power Through Prayer*

———

"The eternal God is your refuge,
and underneath are the everlasting arms..."

-Deuteronomy 33:27

Oct. 20, 2002 - Answer to Prayer

You prayed for my friend G., who had a mastectomy almost a year ago. Because of her lupus, she was not able to have Chemo.

She did have Radiotherapy in Dec. / Jan. and suffered for nearly six months afterwards, with burning, lumps/boils/abscesses, and extreme tiredness. They normally give iodine to alleviate these symptoms, but she is allergic to iodine, and so couldn't be given it.

She visited her Oncologist in August, and he said she is fine. Praise the Lord!

Many thanks! -Sophia (Israel)

———

"We foolish mortals sometimes live through years not realizing
how short life is, and that TODAY is your life."

"People throw away what they could have
by insisting on perfection, which they cannot have,
and looking for it where they will never find it."

-Edith Schaeffer (1914-2013)
Author: *L'Abri*; Married to Francis A. Schaeffer

Oct. 24, 2002 - Prayer Request:

Please pray that the law enforcement agents will catch the killer on the loose in the areas surrounding Washington, D.C. This murderer has been shooting and killing innocent people in the nation's Capital since October 9, and the toll is rising. Today he threatened to go after children. Please pray for divine intervention; for an army of angels to surround this killer, and hand him over to law enforcement authorities. We need prayer to stop him. -Thank you.

Answer To Prayer - Oct. 24, 2002 (The Same Day.)

The 23-Day Sniper Shooting / Murder Spree ended today, with the arrest of *two* murderers: an American Black Muslim, and a Jamaican National (13 persons shot: ten dead).

Oct. 28, 2003 - Answer to Prayer:

A couple of weeks ago I asked you to pray for an elderly man in our church; critically ill with bacterial meningitis. Well, I just got an email, and today he is being moved to Rehab! Praise the Lord!! Thank you for praying.

Also, my best friend, Everdine, is now pregnant with her first child, after the doctors told her and her husband Jan that it was impossible for them to have children. After much prayer, they now are expecting a child, which is a true miracle.

Blessings, -Mirjam (Netherlands)

"Lord, the task is impossible for me, but not for Thee.
Lead the way, I will follow.""

"The secret of all failure is disobedience."

"Prayer is the greatest power God has put into our hands for service
-- praying is harder than doing, at least I have found it so,
but the dynamic lies that way to advance the kingdom."

-Mary Slessor (1848-1915)
Scottish Missionary to Calabar (Nigeria)

Oct. 29, 2002 - Answer to Prayer:

Praise report!!!!!!! I discovered my son was indeed depressed... and didn't say anything to me until last night. We spoke at length and prayed together. We re-dedicated our lives to Jesus, and asked the Lord to please draw us nearer to Him, and help us to trust Him more in all things, and to keep our focus on Him and not our circumstances.

All of a sudden, the Holy Spirit broke loose, and a feeling of Joy and Jubilation came over my son and I, and even over my 84 yr. old mother, who lives with us. My son was feeling better than he has in months. Restoration has come from this in a most miraculous way for our family, and I wanted to share it with all who have been praying. Hallelujah!! Glory to God! There is much Power In Prayer!!!!

Thank you from deep within my heart for your prayers; so that I could see the revelation the Lord has given to me about growing in trust, and placing my focus on Him, and asking Him to help me with those things, instead of meeting circumstantial needs. I love you, Jesus. :) Love in Christ, -Sister Joyce + (California)

Dec. 9, 2002 – Answer to Prayer:

I want to thank you all for praying for my daughter, D. She is so much better. I just moved her out here to California with me. She still has a few medical miracles to achieve, but she's doing great. We have truly been blessed. I thank the Lord; and people like you, who continuously pray for all people.

-Sister Joyce + (California)

Elizabeth Elliott spent her life as a Missionary among the Tribe that murdered her 29 year-old Missionary husband.

"This hard place in which you perhaps find yourself is the very place in which God is giving you the opportunity to look only to Him..."

-Elizabeth Elliott (1926-2015) Missionary in Ecuador

Dec. 30, 2002 - Prayer Request:

Please pray for guardian angels to surround P., as he travels back to the west coast. Pray for him to arrive back there safe, alive, and healthy.

God bless. -Jane

Answer to Prayer - Dec. 31, 2002 (One Day Later.)

Praise the Lord! P. returned home safely.

God bless you, and thank you for praying. -Jane

Feb. 27, 2003 – Answer to Prayer:

Thank God it's finally over, after three months of worrying about this gland, the final report came back today from the surgical biopsy and it's negative for Cancer. This gland was painless, with irregular borders, and had a point on one end. The radiologist was very, very concerned, and scared me like crazy.

I started thinking how radically my life would change with a diagnosis of Cancer. When they wanted to do the surgical biopsy, I was terrified of it, and didn't want to do it because of the anesthesia (twilight sleep). I wanted to see spring…well, it's warm out, and the daffodils are in bloom. God is faithful. The surgery was a breeze; I had no fear going in the O.R., and I knew the Lord would take care of me. Praise Him, Praise Him, Praise Him!

I also know the Lord spoke to me when it first was made known, and told me it was nothing, still I allowed fear and doubt to creep in, but He is so faithful. I don't know what that thing was, but I do know this, the Lord took care of it and *all* we ever have to do is trust Him totally. *Praise The Lord, His Mercy Endureth Forever.*

God bless you, and thank you for praying. Our prayers indeed have been answered. Believe Him, believe Him, believe Him; He truly can be trusted.

A Song of Ascents.

From the depths I have cried out to You, O LORD.
LORD, hear my voice.
Let Your ears give attention to the sound of my supplications.
If You LORD, should record our wicked deeds,
O LORD, who could stand before You?
But there is forgiveness with You,
so that we might learn to reverence You.
I wait for the LORD; my soul waits, and in His word I hope.
My soul waits for the LORD;
more than those who watch for the morning.
Let Israel hope in the LORD, for with the LORD is mercy, and
abundant redemption.
God shall redeem Israel from all their transgressions.

-Psalm 130

LORD, my heart is not proud, or my eyes haughty;
I do not concern myself in great matters,
or in things too wonderful for me.

Surely, I have calmed and quieted myself,
like a child who is weaned from his mother.

My soul is like a child who is content.

Let Israel hope in the LORD;
from this day forward,
and forever.

-Psalm 131

"Worship and worry cannot live in the same heart:
they are mutually exclusive."

"We cannot pray and remain the same."

-Ruth Bell Graham (1920-2007) Born in China
Daughter of Medical Missionary Dr. Nelson Bell
Married to World Evangelist Billy Graham

4.4 Needs Met, Husband & Wife Reconciled, Son Hired

*"God answers our prayers not because we are good,
but because He is good."*

-A.W. (Aiden Wilson) Tozer (1897-1963)
Evangelist, Pastor, Theologian
Christian & Missionary Alliance
Author: *The Knowledge of the Holy*

———

*"If two of you shall agree on earth
as touching anything that they shall ask,
it shall be done for them by My Father,
who is in Heaven."*

-Matthew 18:19

Mar. 26, 2003 - Prayer Request:

Please pray that I get my paycheck today, and that we get the money from our loan on Monday. Please pray I get more sponsors, and my biopsy is negative.

God is so faithful; we signed the settlement today, and we're waiting to get one debt cleared. They were supposed to call yesterday, but didn't; pray they get it cleared today!

Thank you and God bless you. Praise the Lord!! -Jane

Answer to Prayer - Mar. 28, 2003 (Two Days Later.)

Praise Report!! Thank God I got paid much needed funds today; I know He brought them, thank you for praying!! God is awesome and right on time!! Also: Praise the Lord, we finally settled our refinancing on our home and we will have some of the equity for bills. I will also be getting my paycheck, praise God!

It's been a tough month, but God is so faithful, *every* need we have had, has been more than met.

My husband's health continues to improve from the heart attack, and I am doing well, also. I need to quit smoking; please pray for me. God bless you, and thank you for praying. God will do it; that's what He says, and that's what He means!! -Jane

---

Apr. 7, 2003 - Prayer Request:

My wife still won't reconcile with me, so please be in agreement with me for God's will in this situation. Amen! -Edward (California)

Answer to Prayer - Apr. 18, 2003 (11 Days Later.)

Praise God! My ex-wife re-dedicated herself to the Lord, is asking me to read the Bible with her, and we are praying together. I'm continuing to stand in prayer for reconciliation as God changes me.
-Edward (California)

Answer to Prayer Update - Apr. 27, 2003 (Nine Days Later.)

My ex-wife attended church today, and is starting to pray and be conscious of the Lord's power and presence.
-Edward (California)

Answer to Prayer Update - May 1, 2003 (Four Days Later.)

I have an awesome praise report! Today as I was dropping off my ex-wife at work, before I went to work, she stated that I could move back in June as a "roommate," on the condition that we continue to attend church services twice weekly. I started to cry, as I realized that God's hand was in her decision.

-Edward (California)

"How many there are...who imagine that because Jesus paid it all, they need pay nothing, forgetting that the prime object of their salvation was that they should follow in the footsteps of Jesus Christ in bringing back a lost world to God."

-Lottie Moon (1840-1912)
Southern Baptist Missionary to China

May 1, 2003 - Prayer Request:

Please pray for my ex-wife to find a new job as her co-workers and boss are being hostile to her; she doesn't go along with their distasteful and obscene jokes and childish behavior. Please keep praying for both of us, and for our children and three grandchildren.

-Edward (California)

Answer to Prayer - May 9, 2003 (Eight Days Later.)

Praise God…my family out there in Christ. My ex-wife and I have reconciled, and we are praying for the needs of others. Also, she was transferred to another location with the same employer, and given full-time hours. In addition, our grandson is safely home after visiting his teen-age father for a week, in a town four hours away from our home.

God is truly an awesome and loving God! -Edward (California)

May 18, 2003 - Prayer Request:

Please pray for my husband, who is having heart surgery tomorrow morning; they are putting in a second stent. Pray for God's grace and favor upon him, and for him to completely be healed and come home quickly. Please also pray for my son to get work; he has a family, and is a believer. God is so good, I thank Him for meeting every need we have. Praise His Holy Name! -Jane

Answer to Prayer - May 20, 2003 (Two Days Later.)

My husband did great, this stent was already ordered after the last one. They found another blockage then, but had to wait for the first one to heal, before they could go in again. He's doing fine, thanks for praying. God bless, -Jane

Answer to Prayer - May 26, 2003 (Six Days Later.)

I've asked you to pray for my son to get his job back from the lay-off, or get a new job. Praise the Lord, he interviewed today for a job; they offered it, and are now negotiating salary. -Jane

---

A Song of Ascents.

LORD, remember David, and all his gentleness.
How he swore an oath to the LORD,
and made a vow to the Mighty One of Jacob:
"Surely I will not go into my palace and up to my bed;
I will not give sleep to my eyes or slumber to my eyelids;
not until I find a place for the LORD,
a habitation for the Mighty One of Jacob."

We heard of the Ark at Ephratah.
We found it in the fields by the groves of trees.
We will go into His Tabernacle. We will worship at His footstool.
Arise, O LORD, into Your rest; You, and the Ark of Your strength.
Let Your priests be clothed with righteousness,
and let Your saints shout for joy.

For your servant David's sake,
do not turn away the face of Your Messiah.
The LORD has sworn this truth to David; He will not turn from it:
"I will set one of your descendants on your throne.
If your children will keep my covenant,
and my laws that I shall teach them,
their children shall also sit on your throne forever."

For the LORD has chosen Zion.
He has desired it for His dwelling place, saying,
"This is my place of rest forever.
Here I will dwell, for I have desired it.
I will bless Jerusalem with abundant provisions.
I will satisfy its poor with bread.
I will also clothe its priests with salvation,
and its saints shall shout for joy.

There I will make the rod of David's power to sprout a Branch.
I have ordained a Lamp for my Messiah.
His enemies I will clothe with shame,
but on Him His crown of holiness shall flourish."

-Psalm 132

David's Branch is Christ. *Messiah's Lamp* is John the Baptist.

96

4.5 *Prayer Warrior* Comments

I was fortunate to have been raised in a church-going home. I accepted Christ as my personal savior at age nine, and was active in youth choir throughout High School. My most memorable experience during this period, was when I took part in a mission trip to Belize. Only in recent months have I realized the importance of daily meditation and prayer in the morning, and scriptural reading and prayer each evening. I will continue to remember the *PrayerFoundation* ™ and its *Prayerchain* requests during my prayer time, with special emphasis on doing so during my Wednesday night prayers.

In Christ, -Brother Eddie (Texas)

Hello & best regards. I have been Christian since always I was a child. I did fall away in teen years, but God did touch my heart when I was 20 years old.

I have beautiful 10 years old girl, she wonderful God's gift. I live in Iceland. I have walk with this desire become a Lay Monk. I know that is rare today, but this much be calling on my life. I love my Lord Jesus with all of my heart.

God bless you, -Johann H. (Reykjavik, Iceland)

I have been enjoying the discipline of *Praying the Hours*. Thanks. I am also enjoying the website and participating as a *Prayer Warrior*. God's blessing of increase and influence be upon all of you. For the Kingdom!!!

-Pastor Bernie (Ontario, Canada)

"Never be afraid to trust an unknown future to a known God."

*"Worry does not empty tomorrow of its sorrow;
it empties today of its strength."*

-Corrie ten Boom (1892-1983) Dutch. Interred in Ravensbruck Concentration Camp for aiding Jews to escape the Nazis.

4.6 The Psalms

"We have now before us one of the choicest parts of the Old Testament, wherein there is so much of Christ and His Gospel, as well as of God and His Law, that it has been called the summary of both Testaments."

-Matthew Henry (1662-1714) English Nonconformist Minister
Author: *Exposition of the Old and New Testaments* (6 Vol.)

———

*"The Psalter is the great school of prayer...
The more deeply we grow into the psalms
and the more often we pray them as our own,
the more simple and rich our prayer will become."*

-Dietrich Bonhoeffer (1906-1945) German Lutheran Pastor
Theologian, Martyr; Author: *The Cost of Discipleship*
and *Psalms: The Prayer Book of the Bible*

———

"When we read the Psalms, we are meant to learn things about God and about human nature and about how life is to be lived."

-John Piper, Author: *Desiring God* and *Don't Waste Your Life*

———

"The Psalmists in telling everyone to praise God are doing what all men do when they speak of what they care about."

-C.S. Lewis (1898-1963) Author: *Reflections on the Psalms*

———

"The delightful study of the Psalms has yielded me boundless profit and ever-growing pleasure;
common gratitude constrains me to communicate to others a portion of the benefit, with the prayer that it may induce them to search further for themselves."

-Charles Spurgeon (1834-1892) "The Prince of Preachers"
Author: *The Treasury of David* (Commentary On the Psalms)

* * *

4.7 Dear *PrayerFoundation* ™

Dear Brethren, greetings in Christ our Lord. I am a minister in the *Presbyterian Church in America*... I have enjoyed your website over the past few years, and have profited from it.

I am particularly interested in praying the Psalms. I have read your article by Athanasius: *Letter to Marcellinus* (*On Praying the Psalms*), and enjoyed it.

In Christ, -Richard H.

Thank you so much -- God Bless You All,

-Ariane (Belgium)

I trust in God: I know He will deliver because Jesus said so.

-Manuel J. (Peru)

England needs many prayers at the moment because not many people believe in Jesus here anymore.

I feel I am being called by God to be a Lay Monk and be a man of God. I am very interested in prayer, spend many times a day praying, and hope to help your ministry with prayer and action.

-Dominic W. (U.K.)

Thank you, to all intercessors.

-James W. (Kenya)

"I will cling to Christ like a burr on a topcoat."

"I've read enough, I've heard enough, I know enough.
Would to God I lived it."

-Katharina Von Bora / "Katie" Luther (1499-1552)
Former Cistercian Nun; Married to Martin Luther

Dear friends, I'm an English language teacher from Scotland currently working / living in Estonia. I have been quite actively Christian for many years and have now come to a stage in my life where I feel a need to do more with and for my spiritual growth.

I have read your website many times and have come to the conclusion that it is the right way forward for me at this stage in my life...to join your Order as a Lay Monk, so that I may fulfill God's plan for me and this wonderful gift He gave us all...life. Best wishes and God bless,

-Martin P. (Estonia; originally from Scotland)

My name is Chris from Bangor in County Down, N. Ireland. I am a Protestant minister (ordained as an evangelist). Over 10 years ago myself and an Augustinian Brother formed an Order called the *Heart of St. Patrick.* I guess it was our way of responding to a post-conflict Ulster which had stereotyped the Scriptures / the Good News.

On looking at your website, we seem to have so much in common -- a passion for Christ, ecumenical for the Gospel's sake, itinerant, evangelistic. We often joke that we seek to glorify God by doing as much damage to the devil with as little collateral damage to people.

Thanks for being there, -Chris (Bangor, County Down, N. Ireland)

Dear Lay Monks, Thank you for the wonderful (and beautiful) E-Newsletter. I have long been a reader of your website, and have been blessed many times by the writings there. I wanted to take just a few moments to send you my thanks, and prayers of blessings and peace.

-Rev. Roger (*Christ Church Mission*)

Dear Brethren and Sisters in Christ, thanks for your great Site. Blessings in Him,

-Sr. Brigid <(((><

S.G. Preston

After so long I have, by God's grace, stumbled across your door. Where have you been, or where have I been? Many times I have told persons that my calling is to encourage people to deepen their prayer lives, to grow in the intimacy of their relationship with God -- Father, Son and Holy Spirit.

I am among those who question if we had missed our path by not being a member of a monastic Order. I have spent half days and one overnight at *St. Bernard's Monastery* in *Alabama*. I just asked her and she confirms that I am *a monk at heart*, to which she added, "Of course no one will understand."

-Robert (Alabama)

Re: Newsletter. Thought you guys forgot about us. Good to hear from you. -Rev. Br. Larry (*Franciscan Lutheran Community Chapel*; Florida)

Greetings of peace in Jesus' holy name. I saw your webpages and found them inspiring. I'm a Secular Franciscan (Third Order) for close to fifty years. Thank you. God bless...

-R.J.R., SFO

Lay Monk Preston and Lay Monk Linda, Greetings, and may God continue to shine His glorious light upon you and your organization. I just returned to California about a week ago from Australia. I plan to return there permanently between six months and a year from now. My chosen field of study is Historical Theology, and the planned subject for my Doctoral Thesis is: *"The Emergence of Protestant Monasticism in the 20th Century."* I believe that your group is doing some marvelous work. I just want to say thank you for a job well done, and wish you continued success.

I will keep you and your group in my prayers, and I ask God's blessings on all. -Rev. Philip E. (California / Australia)

"Love Him totally, who gave Himself totally for your love."

"We become what we love,
and who we love shapes what we become.
If we love things, we become a thing.
If we love nothing, we become nothing.

Imitation is not a literal mimicking of Christ,
rather it means becoming the image of the beloved,
an image disclosed through transformation.

This means we are to become vessels
of God's compassionate love for others."

-St. Clare of Assisi (1194-1253 A.D.)
Co-Founder (With St. Francis) of the *Poor Clares*

———

Gladys Aylward was called by God to the Mission Field of China. An English Housemaid with no education, she was turned down by all of the Missionary Organizations. She paid her own way to China, knowing no one there, and having no Mission-sponsored support.

The inspiring Hollywood Movie about her life's work is called *The Inn of the Sixth Happiness*, and stars Ingrid Bergman as Gladys. It's a *Must See!*

"Oh God, here's my Bible, here's my money.
Here's me. Use me, God."

"These are my people, God has given them to me,
and I will live or die for Him and His glory."

"I wasn't God's first choice for what I've done in China...
I don't know who it was...it must have been a man...
a well-educated man. I don't know what happened.

Perhaps he died. Perhaps he wasn't willing...
and God looked down...and saw Gladys Aylward...
and God said, 'Well, she's willing.'"

-Gladys Aylward (1902-1970) Missionary to China

4.8 Gregory, Gregory, and Basil

"Christ is the artist,
tenderly wiping away all the grime of sin
that disfigures the human face
and restoring God's image
to its full beauty."

-St. Gregory of Nyssa (c. 335-c. 395 A.D.)

———

"The first of all beautiful things
is the continual possession of God.

"It is more important that we should remember God
than that we should breathe;
indeed, if one may say so,
we should do nothing else besides."

"Let us treasure up in our soul some of those things which are
permanent...not of those which will forsake us and be destroyed,
and which only tickle our senses for a little while."

"Let us not esteem worldly prosperity or adversity as things real
or of any moment, but let us live elsewhere,
and raise all our attention to Heaven;
esteeming sin as the only true evil, and nothing truly good,
but virtue which unites us to God."

-St. Gregory of Nazianzus (c. 329-390 A.D.).

———

"Words are truly the image of the soul."

"We should not express our prayer merely in syllables,
but the power of prayer should be expressed in the moral attitude of
our soul and in the virtuous actions that extend throughout our life...

This is how you pray continually -- not by offering prayer in words,
but by joining yourself to God through your whole way of life, so
that your life becomes one continuous and uninterrupted prayer."

-St. Basil the Great (329-379 A.D.)

4.9 Lay Monk Thoughts: Kindness

*"A tree is known by its fruit; a man by his deeds.
A good deed is never lost; he who sows courtesy reaps friendship,
and he who plants kindness, gathers love."*

-St. Basil the Great (329-379 A.D.)

---

*"But the fruit of the Spirit is love, joy, peace,
patience, kindness, goodness,
faithfulness, gentleness, self-control."*

-Galatians 5:22-23

**"Those who are kind benefit themselves; but those
who are cruel hurt themselves." -Proverbs 11:27**

We are to do all things in love. *"God is love."* -1 John 4:8,16

*"Love is patient and kind; love does not envy or boast;
it is not arrogant or rude. It does not insist on its own way;
it is not irritable or resentful; it does not rejoice at wrongdoing,
but rejoices with the truth."* -1 Corinthians 13:4-6

*"A righteous person has regard for the life of his animals,
but even the mercies of the wicked are cruel."* -Proverbs 12:10

As Christians we are to be kind and practice kindness.
**St. Francis and the ancient Celtic Christian Monks loved
animals.** On October 4, St. Francis' Feast Day, many Churches will
bless your pets. The Roman Catholic Church has designated St.
Francis as the Patron Saint of Animals (and of Ecology).

In England in 1824, member of Parliament William Wilberforce
was one of the Founders of the first animal welfare society: the *Royal
Society for the Prevention of Cruelty to Animals*.

* * *

104

5. *LORD God Almighty (El Shaddai)*

5.1 Infections Cleared Up, Pet Healed, Given Salary Bonus

*"We are to pray in times of adversity,
lest we become faithless and unbelieving.*

*We are to pray in times of prosperity,
lest we become boastful and proud.*

*We are to pray in times of danger,
lest we become fearful and doubting.*

*We are to pray in times of security,
lest we become self-sufficient."*

-Billy Graham (1918-2018)

———

*"Rejoice always. Pray without ceasing. In everything give thanks.
For this is the will of God in Christ Jesus concerning you.
Do not quench the Spirit."*

-1 Thessalonians 5:16-19

Nov. 12, 2003 - Answer to Prayer:

I asked you to pray for Ann, who was going for an examination for a nodule in her breast. Just got a call from her and she is fine; no Cancer, no problem!!!

-(California)

---

*"Here is the principle - adapt your measures to the
necessity of the people to whom you minister.
You are to take the Gospel to them in such modes
and circumstances as will gain for it
from them a hearing."*

-Catherine Booth (1829-1890)
Co-Founder of *The Salvation Army*

Nov. 16, 2003 - Answer to Prayer:

A few weeks ago, I asked you to pray for Clifford, who is in an Arizona hospital, and was at death's door. He was eaten up with infection and Cancer, and couldn't eat or keep food down; the doctors gave him little or no hope a few weeks ago. Tonight I got a call, and Clifford is eating solid food, and keeping it down. His infection, that left big holes in his body, has cleared up, and some are saying he's on the road to recovery! God bless you, and thank you for praying.

Love, -Jane (California)

Nov. 27, 2003 - Prayer Request:

Please pray for my seven year-old daughter, as she has been suffering from an acute ear infection over a week now, and is losing weight rapidly. Her name is Cassidy. God bless you all.

-Barbie (Washington State)

Answer to Prayer (The Same Day.) Received Dec. 10, 2003

Dear *Prayer Warriors*, Thank you all so much for praying for my little daughter, who was so sick, and growing weak and thin. I want to tell you that *the very day* I e-mailed in my urgent request, Cassidy made an abrupt turn-around, and climbed steadily back into health. She is now completely well, fattening up again with rosy cheeks. Our God is good!!! -Barbie (Washington State)

Nov. 30, 2003 - Answer to Prayer (Two Days Later.)

Thanks to those who joined us in prayer for our Monk-Cat Tigré, who suddenly began breaking out in lesions and was not responding to antibiotics. She is now completely healed; only two days after all of you started praying! -Lay Monk Linda (Portland, Oregon)

Dec. 14, 2003 - Prayer Request:

Please pray for little C., she is having problems getting her bowels to move. She is on medication, but it is working very slowly. She is a toddler, and she also has a viral infection. Please pray for total healing. Pray for wisdom and good judgment for her parents, regarding this situation. God is able, *Praise His Holy Name.*

106

S.G. Preston

Answer to Prayer - Dec. 17, 2003 (Three Days Later.)

Praise the Lord! Little C. is much better. She had a big bowel movement, and her mother has decided to keep her on the medication a little longer. Her cold is better, too. This one is a nasty virus, it wants to hang on; been fighting it myself. God bless you, and thank you for praying.

Dec. 6, 2004 - Answer to Prayer:

Praise the Lord Jesus! Many thanks to you, for all the fervent *prayers* you have offered up to the Almighty God on behalf of me. It gives me great *joy* to tell you that the Almighty God has been showering his abundant *blessings* upon me, because of your fervent *prayers*. Those in authority have given me permission to take holiday every Saturday.

Well, another great blessing that the Almighty God has showered upon me, is that he has touched the hearts of all those in authority, and as a result of this, they have given me the entire salary of 2,000 rupees for the whole month, when I have worked there only for 15 days.

The one who gave me the salary said, "This is our Christmas gift to you." Although I am delayed in the Office, because the vehicles are not available, or the drivers are not available; yet because of God's divine favour, arrangements are made to drop me back home by the company's own vehicle, itself.

Well, I am still learning the extension board numbers, and trying to learn each and every thing pertaining to Telephone Operating.

-Sandra (India)

Dec. 20, 2003 - Answer to Prayer:

Thank you so much, for praying for Bobby with the brain tumor. I just got a card, and his mother-in-law is saying he is much better, thanks to the prayers from all of you.

107

The Martyrdom of Perpetua and Felicity (203 A.D.)

The last words of Perpetua, as testified to
by the eyewitnesses of her martyrdom:

*"Stand fast in the faith, and love one another, all of you,
and be not offended at my sufferings."*

Perpetua and Felicity were executed by wild beasts with several
other Christians at the Arena in Carthage on March 7, 203 A.D.
This execution of several Christians by Bull, Bear, and Leopard was
held to celebrate the Emperor Septimus Severus' birthday.
Much of the account we have was written in Latin by Perpetua
herself, one of the earliest pieces of writing by a Christian woman.

**She was a nobly born, educated twenty-two year old married
woman, with a new baby, and was arrested with the servant
Felicity, who was with child (her baby was born before her
execution). Both were arrested for the Capital Crime of merely
being a Christian.** Perpetua and Felicity were Catechumens
preparing for baptism and were baptized a few days before being
taken to prison.

Perpetua's father visited her in the prison, begging her:

*"Spare your father's gray hairs; spare the infancy of the boy.
Make sacrifice for the Emperor's prosperity."
And I answered: "I am a Christian."*

They were to be dressed in robes of pagan goddess priestesses for
their execution, and when they refused to do so, the enraged crowd
demanded that they also be scourged with whips before being killed.

**Perpetua, mauled by the beast and covered in blood, had not
died, so a Gladiator approached her with a sword:**
*"Perpetua was pierced between the bones and shrieked out; and
when the swordsman's hand wandered (for he was still a novice),
herself set it upon her own neck. Perchance so great a woman
could not else have been slain (being feared by the unclean spirit)
had she herself not willed it."*

3rd Century Quotations taken from:
The Passion of Saints Perpetua and Felicity (Transl. by Tertullian)

5.2 Retained Custody, Missing Son Found, Surgery Canceled

*"The story of every great Christian achievement
is the history of answered prayer."*

-E.M. Bounds (1835-1913) Methodist Pastor
Author: *Power Through Prayer*

———

*"For where two or three are gathered together in My name,
there am I in the midst of them."*

-Matthew 18:20

Jan. 11, 2003 - Prayer Request:

Once again, I come to you for prayer in your group. I had a mammogram last week, a follow-up from 7 months ago. At that time, I had a swollen gland under my arm, and the doctor said it was nothing. I had them look at it again this week with ultra-sound, and now they say it's something, and I need a biopsy. Please pray that there is nothing seriously wrong. I know the devil is just trying to shake me up. Too bad: God is in control, and I know He will bring me though this victoriously. Thank you, and God bless.
  -Jane (Virginia)

Answer to Prayer - Jan. 22, 2002 (Eleven Days Later.)

They did not find any Cancer in my biopsy!! Praise the Lord!! They still want me to have it removed, to be absolutely sure, but I'm already absolutely sure. God is awesome, and I know this is OK. Praise His Holy Name!! Thank you for praying…and keep it up, please. -Jane (Virginia)

———

*"You can set up an altar to God in your minds by means of prayer.
And so it is fitting to pray at your trade, on a journey,
standing at a counter or sitting at your handicraft."*

St. John Chrysostom (347-407 A.D.) Martyr

109

Jan. 23, 2003 - Prayer Request:

Please pray for our son Brandon to return home to us as soon as possible. Tomorrow at 9:30 a.m. in Ontario, Canada, we have a custody trial. We spent five years fighting for him, and had custody. We don't know what happened, but Brandon is saying he wants to be with his mother - yet only a few weeks ago he never wanted to see her ever. Brandon does not belong there - she has 10 kids, all from different fathers, and uses the children for her income: welfare, baby bonus, child support, etc.

She has been manipulating and psychologically abusing Brandon and the other children. Please pray Brandon makes the right decision, and God guides him back home, where he is truly loved and wanted...he just had his 11th birthday and this is when his mother kept him. I am so scared of losing Brandon...and for his future. Please pray for us. Bless all of you, -Jacqueline (Ontario, Canada)

Answer to Prayer - Jan. 31, 2003 (Eight Days Later.)

Thank you, our prayers have been answered.
God Bless You, -Jacqueline (Ontario, Canada)

Feb. 5, 2003 - Answer to Prayer:

I am seeing the impact of your prayers, and give the glory to God. Thanks very much for your effort and love.
Remain blessed, -(Nigeria)

Feb. 6, 2003 - Answer to Prayer:

Thank you for praying for me for so long; I finally got a great job! -(Oregon)

June 22, 2003 - Answer to Prayer:

The woman whose son was missing for more than a month -- he has been found. He is well. -God bless you, and *Praise the Lord* for answered prayer!

June 23, 2003 - Prayer Request:

Grandma is doing very well. The Cancer seems to be gone completely. Herman is alright as well. He had his last seizure on May 4, in the early afternoon.

When he came out of the seizure, he found himself sitting on the sofa. He has no idea what he had been doing in the meantime, or how long he had been there. -Mirjam (Netherlands)

June 27, 2003 - Answer to Prayer:

Yesterday we paid the mortgage company every dime of what we owed. We had to count change to do it, but God provided every dime of it in two days!!! -(California)

Sept. 19, 2003 - Prayer Request:

Please pray for Tom. He broke his arm six months ago, and it is not healing. His Doctor says they will have to perform surgery.

-Robert (Washington State)

Oct. 9, 2003 - Answer to Prayer (One Month Later.)

Keep praying for Tom's arm, which had not been healing from a break for over six months, but began healing when your *Prayerchain* began praying for him.

Thanks so much. -Robert (Washington State)

Oct. 17, 2003 - Answer to Prayer Update (Eight Days Later.)

The Doctors said Tom still needed surgery, because his arm was only ten percent healed. When Tom went in for his surgery, they did a preliminary X-ray, and his Doctor was shocked, because the arm was 80% healed! The Surgeon canceled Tom's surgery, saying it was no longer necessary! Tom's healing is truly a miracle! Thank you so much, all of you who were praying.

-Robert (Washington State)

Sept. 30, 2003 - Answer to Prayer:

My daughter-in-law and I went out today, and when I came home there was a nice sizable check in my mail, *totally unexpected*, from someone I had done some work for last year. I had invoiced them for extra work, but then they said they changed their mind. Anyway, they paid it today!!!

"The chief danger that confronts the coming century
will be religion without the Holy Ghost,
Christianity without Christ,
forgiveness without repentance,
salvation without regeneration,
politics without God,
heaven without hell."

"'Not called' did you say?
'Not heard the call,' I think you should say.

Put down your ear to the Bible,
and hear Him bid you go and pull sinners out of the fire of sin.
Put your ear down to the burdened, agonized heart of humanity,
and listen to its pitiful wail for help.

Go stand by the gates of hell and hear the damned entreat you
to go to their father's house and bid their brothers and sisters
and servants and masters not to come there.

Then look Christ in the face --
whose mercy you have professed to obey --
and tell Him whether you will join heart and soul
and body and circumstances in the march
to publish His mercy to the world."

-William Booth (1829-1912)

"If we are to better the future, we must disturb the present."

-Catherine Booth (1829-1990) Co-Founder
with her husband William: *The Salvation Army*

112

5.3 No Hope: Healed, Not Fired / Gets Raise, Now Can Have Child

"Beware in your prayers, above everything else,
of limiting God, not only by unbelief,
but by fancying that you know
what He can do.

Expect unexpected things 'above all that we
ask or think.'"

-Andrew Murray (1828-1917)
Author: *With Christ in the School of Prayer*

———

"Be filled with care about nothing;
but in everything by prayer and supplication,
with thanksgiving, let your requests
be made known to God.

And the peace of God,
which passes all understanding,
shall keep your hearts and minds
through Christ Jesus."

-Philippians 4:6-7

Oct. 1, 2003 - Answer to Prayer:

My husband had his stress test today and it went fine, he is doing so well after having a heart attack in March. So far little or no damage to his heart. Praise the Lord! -(California)

"Thanksgiving is inseparable from true prayer;
it is almost essentially connected with it.
One who always prays is ever giving praise,
whether in ease or pain, both for prosperity
and for the greatest adversity."

-John Wesley (1703-1791) Founder: *Methodists*

Oct. 13, 2003 - Answer to Prayer (Two Weeks Later.)

A couple of weeks ago I asked you to pray for Larry, near death and needing a lung transplant. He had waited and waited. I just got a phone call; Larry had the transplant, and is doing beautifully. A second person also had a transplant with the other lung, and he too is doing very well. Praise the Lord!!! Praise His Holy Name!!

God bless.

Dec. 31, 2007 - Answer to Prayer:

Greetings in Jesus' Name.

1.) Two months back three managers (including my own manager) tried to sack me from my job, but after much prayers and by God's Immense Grace, that did not materialize, and I am still in the same company.

2.) I got a promotion and pay hikes this year.

3.) God has blessed us with a second girl baby as a Christmas gift, and also a normal delivery; and good health for my wife.

4.) God gave us admission for my first kid to our preferred school.

Thanking You,

   -(Washington State)

Jan. 21, 2004 – Answer to Prayer:

As you know, Jeff had to go in for what I thought was a surgical biopsy for his esophagus today. He went in, they used the anesthesia, then they took a look with a tube down his throat and through his esophagus. *They Found Nothing!!!!*

Praise the Lord, the whole procedure was over within an hour and a half, and he's fine and breathing a deep sigh of relief. I told him of my prayer request for him, and he was so pleased. He is a strong believer, and very thankful to God and to you for praying, as am I, his mom. God bless you and thank you so much. -Jane (California)

114

S.G. Preston

Jan. 29, 2004 - Answer to Prayer:

Thanks be to Jesus, I was called for my new job today. I lost my last job due to an injury. I have been out of work almost two years. Thank you, Jesus.

Feb. 11, 2004 - Answer to Prayer:

Praise the Lord Jesus...Alleluia, Many thanks to you for all the fervent prayers you have offered up to the Almighty God on behalf of my mother. Well, the operation has already been performed, and she has been kept under observation. She will return home in the evening.

With your prayers, peace descended upon each one of us in the home, and deep down in my heart, I have the assurance all is well. Thanks once again for all your fervent prayers.

Yours in Christ always, -Sandra (India)

Feb. 20, 2004 - Answer to Prayer:

Thank you very much! ...for praying for a spiritual and financial breakthrough. God is indeed awesome and mighty!

He always fulfills what He promised in His word! We can always depend on His faithfulness to protect and defend us!

-Maria

Mar. 25, 2004 - Prayer Request:

My friend Heather *really* has wanted a child. They have tried many things, and this is the last attempt.

I would like to ask everyone to pray to my Father, that if it is His will, to please help this one to take. And if it is not His will; to please give us the faith that He knows best.

And last, if there is any "wiggle room" can she *please* have this!!

Thanks, *Amen.* -Christopher (Seattle)

Answer to Prayer - Apr. 13, 2004 (Nineteen Days Later.)

First, thanks to God, and to all of you who prayed for my last request, to assist my friend. It appears that this time it worked! Thanks be to God, and thank *all* of you for your prayers.

-Christopher (Seattle)

A Song of Ascents of David.

Behold how good and how pleasant it is,
for brethren to dwell together in unity!

It is like the precious oil upon the head,
that ran down the beard…that ran down Aaron's beard;
the fragrant oil that ran down to the borders of his robe.

It is like the dew of Mount Hermon,
and the dew that descended on the mountains of Zion.
For there the LORD commanded the blessing: even life forever.

-Psalm 133

———

A Song of Ascents.

Behold: bless ye the LORD, all ye servants of the LORD,
which by night, stand in the House of the LORD.

Lift up your hands in the Sanctuary, and bless the LORD.
The LORD, that made heaven and earth, bless thee out of Zion.

-Psalm 134

———

"In a word, live together in the forgiveness of your sins, for without it no human fellowship, least of all a marriage, can survive.
Don't insist on your rights, don't blame each other,
don't judge or condemn each other, don't find fault with each other,
but accept each other as you are, and forgive each other every day
from the bottom of your hearts..."

-Dietrich Bonhoeffer (1906-1945)

116

John Chrysostom On Prayer

"The highest good is prayer and conversation with God, because it means that we are in God's company and in union with Him.
When light enters our bodily eyes our eyesight is sharpened; when a soul is intent on God, God's inextinguishable light shines into it and makes it bright and clear.

I am talking, of course, of prayer that comes from the heart, and not routine: not the prayer that is assigned to particular days or particular moments in time, but the prayer that happens continuously by day and by night.

Indeed the soul should not only turn to God at times of explicit prayer. Whatever we are engaged in, whether it is care for the poor, or some other duty, or some act of generosity, we should remember God and long for God.

The love of God will be as salt to food, making our actions into a perfect dish to set before the Lord of all things.
Then it is right that we should receive the fruits of our labors, overflowing onto us through all eternity, if we have been offering them to Him throughout our lives.

Prayer is the light of the soul, true knowledge of God, a mediator between God and men. Prayer lifts the soul into the heavens where it hugs God in an indescribable embrace. The soul seeks the milk of God like a baby crying for the breast. It fulfills its vows and receives in exchange gifts better than anything that can be seen or imagined.

Prayer is a go-between linking us to God.
It gives joy to the soul and calms its emotions.
I warn you, though: do not imagine that prayer is simply words. Prayer is the desire for God, an indescribable devotion, not given by man, but brought about by God's grace. As St. Paul says:

'For when we cannot choose words in order to pray properly, the Spirit Himself intercedes on our behalf in a way that could never be put into words.'"

-St. John Chrysostom (347-407 A.D.) Martyr

5.4 French Ban Ended, Cancer Healed, India Missionaries Released

*"We have to pray with our eyes on God,
not on the difficulties."*

-Oswald Chambers (1874-1917)

———

*"I have kept my eyes always upon the LORD;
because He is at my right hand, I shall not be overcome."*

-Psalm 16:8

Mar. 29, 2004 - Answer To Prayer:

We here at the *PrayerFoundation* ™ were watching the News today, and heard them announce that Mel Gibson's film, *The Passion of the Christ,* which had been banned from being shown in France, would now be allowed to be seen there. We had reported this ban on our website a month ago, but could find no confirmation of the banning from any other source.

Our own information came to us from Jim Caviezal, the actor who plays Christ in the film, through a friend of his. We could find no other mention of it, either by News sources, or even on Internet postings. Our thanks to those of you who prayed with us for the French ban to be lifted.

  -The Lay Monks (Vancouver, Washington)

———

Apr. 5, 2004 - Answer to Prayer:

I asked you to pray for Jeff; about his job, and for job security, and relief from stress, and about the woman supervisor who has been giving him such a hard time. Well, the Lord is definitely working in this situation, and bringing about miracles. Jeff got a raise in pay, and his stress seems to be greatly reduced. I know this is due to God's blessing and prayer!

  -(California)

Apr. 13, 2004 - Prayer Request:

Today, a friend of mine is having surgery for Colon Cancer. He is in poor health. His surgery is today. I ask that you all pray for him and his family, and that God prepare each of them for what His plan is, and to give us guidance how to manage the family dynamics afterwards. This man's wife had a stroke 10 years ago, and he was her caregiver. If my friend survives today, or if he joins our Father, I know that we as a community have prayed, and confirmed that His will be done. Thanks all of you, and may God bless.

-Christopher (Seattle, Washington)

Answer to Prayer - Apr. 15, 2004

Thank you for your prayers; his surgery went well.
God Bless, -Christopher (Seattle, Washington)

May 3, 2004 - Answer to Prayer:

Herman has not had another relapse of seizures. Herman's Aunt Maartje, was diagnosed with a very aggressive form of lung cancer. She was declared healed some time ago.

God bless you all. -Mirjam (Netherlands)

July 1, 2004 - Answer to Prayer:

I wanted to thank *The Prayer Foundation ™ Prayer Warriors* for praying for myself and my children concerning our camping weekend. My daughter and I especially had some of the deepest, most important talks we've had in a very long time. And since returning home, I've noticed a definite difference between my sons and me.

God is faithful! -Brother Seamus (Ontario, Canada)

July 9, 2004 - Answer to Prayer:

I thank the Lord Jesus Christ for showering blessings upon us, as finally my husband has started his work in Kuwait. -Reema S. (India)

119

Aug. 20, 2004 - Answer to Prayer:

Many thanks to the *Prayer Warriors* for upholding my family and I, during our recent time of loss. My children received the news of their grandmother's death with sadness yes, but also with a great amount of joy because they know she is with Jesus!

The peace of God was strong in our home, and at the funeral. Praise God for the Comforter!

-Brother Seamus (Ontario, Canada)

Sept. 11, 2004 - Prayer Request:

Please pray for native missionary Pastor Manrathan and his wife, and for Bible Distributor Sarita. These folks are Indian Nationals who work with *Gospel For Asia*.

The pastor and his wife have been captured, beaten and threatened with death. Sarita is also being held hostage. The group responsible is the same one that burned alive missionary Graham Staines and his children, a few years ago.

Thank you. -Doug (Ontario, Canada)

Answer to Prayer - Sept. 16, 2004 (Five Days Later.)

Praise God! A good report out of India!

Native missionary Pastor Manrathan and his wife, and Bible lady Sarita, have all been released from bondage.

Though all three were beaten before their release, they have all been returned safe. There is no evidence of the ransom being paid. Upon hearing of this persecution, seventeen other native pastors had gone to the village and spoke with each of the hostage takers.

Though they were met with hostility, they watched as the Spirit of God softened hearts, and within a short time, the decision was made to release the captives.

-Doug (Ontario, Canada)

120

Dec. 5, 2004 - Answer to Prayer:

Dear *Prayer Warriors* in Jesus, I have recently been receiving tremendous healing for the muscles in my neck. They were all knotted up with stuck energy (fear). It felt like a raw nerve ending. I grew up in a violent Alcoholic home. That is the root cause of my illness. I am almost completely healed, praise God and Jesus. I am so happy. All Glory to God and Jesus. I love them so much. And, I love you too, my fellow Christian Warriors in Christ.

May God Bless You Richly, -Darryl (Ontario, Canada)

"Nothing will silence infidels so quickly
as Christians everywhere being united."

-Dwight Moody (1837-1899) World Evangelist
Author: *Prevailing Prayer*

———

"If God give to someone the gift of such prayer, it is a gift of
imperishable riches, a heavenly food that satisfies the spirit.
Whoever tastes that food catches fire and his soul
burns forever with desire for the Lord.

To begin on this path, start by adorning your house with modesty
and humility. Make it shine brightly with the light of justice.
Decorate it with the gold leaf of works, with the jewels of
faithfulness and greatness of heart.

Finally, to make the house perfect,
raise a gable above it all, a gable of prayer.
Thus you will have prepared a pure
and sparkling house for the Lord.

Receive the Lord into this royal and splendid dwelling
-- in other words: receive, by His grace,
His image into the temple of your soul."

-St. John Chrysostom (347-407 A.D.) *"Golden Mouth"*
Monk; Patriarch of Constantinople; Martyr

Dwight Moody On Prayer

"Fiery trials make golden Christians;
sanctified afflictions are spiritual promotions."

———

"If we read the Word and do not pray,
we may become puffed up with knowledge,
without the love that builds up.

If we pray without reading the word,
we shall be ignorant of the mind and will of God,
and become mystical and fanatical,
and liable to be blown about
by every wind of doctrine."

———

"Here we are, getting blessings from God day after day;
yet how little praise and thanksgiving there is in the church."

———

"So when we really get into communion with God,
He lifts up His countenance upon us;
and instead of our having gloomy looks,
our faces will shine, because God has
heard and answered our prayers."

———

"If you get love into your soul, so that the grace of God
may come down in answer to prayer,
there will be no trouble about reaching the people.

It is not by eloquent sermons
that perishing souls are going to be reached;
we need the power of God in order that
the blessing may come down."

-Dwight Moody (1837-1899) World Evangelist
Author: *Prevailing Prayer*

122

5.5 *Prayer Warrior* Comments

I noticed that the last *Country of the Week for Prayer* on the *Prayer Requests* Page was *Georgia*. I plan to lead a team there next year to assist Missionaries to build a Christian School…

I just stumbled onto your website yesterday. How exciting!

About six months ago God called me to go to Seminary for a Masters of Counseling Psychology. Did God direct me to your website? I intend to attend Western Seminary in Portland in September. I would be more than interested in participating in ministry with you, particularly with the *Prayerchain*.

Grace and peace, -Cody (Richland, Washington)

Dear Brothers and Sisters in Christ, I wanted to write and confirm my commitment as a Prayer Warrior. I have reviewed your website with great joy and am using your *Threefold Daily Prayers* in my daily devotions.

I was so impressed with the clarity and simplicity of your plan that I volunteered for the *24-Hr. Prayerchain*.

I reviewed your *Statement of Faith* and found that it meets my spiritual needs perfectly. Your ministry has blessed my life and I am grateful. May the Lord continue to bless your efforts.

Yours in Christ, -Lon E. (Tennesee)

Thank you so much. Yours is a fantastic website; it gives me comfort to read all the answered prayers.

-Jonie (West Virginia)

"Those who have left the deepest impression on this sin-cursed earth have been men and women of prayer."

-Dwight Moody (1837-1899) World Evangelist
Author: *Prevailing Prayer*

5.6 Eight "I Am's" of Christ

"I am the bread of life. Those that come to Me shall never hunger, and those that believe in Me shall never thirst."

-John 6:35

"I am the door of the sheep. All that ever came before Me are thieves and robbers, but the sheep did not hear them."

-John 8:7-8

"I am the light of the world. Those that follow Me shall not walk in darkness, but shall have the light of life."

-John 8:12

"I am the good shepherd. The good shepherd gives his life for the sheep."

-John 10:11

"I am the resurrection and the life. Those that believe in Me, though they were dead, yet shall they live."

-John 11:25

"I am the way, the truth, and the life; no one comes to the Father except through Me."

-John 14:6

"I am the true vine, and My Father is the vinedresser. I am the vine, you are the branches."

-John 15:1

"Before Abraham was born, I AM."

-John 8:58

* * *

5.7 Dear *PrayerFoundation* ™

I praise God for your web site, and for your encouragement to live a holy life in conduct and prayer. And I have found the information and videos on the great Celtic saints of the early dark ages most helpful. Last year my wife and I followed the trail of Cuthbert from Melrose to Lindisfarne Island and ultimately to Durham Cathedral, the final resting place of his body.

I see you stand for the holy freedom we have in Christ, after reading Lay Monk Linda's testimony.

In Christ, -James M. (Virginia)

_____

I genuinely want to learn more and I think this ministry could profoundly help shape my soul to help me become more like our Savior. Thank you again. I truly appreciate your quick and kind reply.

Blessings, -Kevin P. (San Antonio, Texas)

_____

Dear Brethren, I wrote to you some time ago to tell you what a blessing your ministry has been to me, and the same is still the case. I have been enjoying your website for years, probably since it was fairly new. I really like the prayer schedule of *The Threefold Daily Prayers.*

In Christ, -Rev. Richard H.

_____

Dear Saints in Christ, please pray for us.

-Raaji (India)

_____

"My experience is that those who pray most in their closets generally make short prayers in public."

-Dwight Moody (1837-1899) World Evangelist
Author: *Prevailing Prayer*

I've been rattling around on this planet for half a century now. I'm married to the same precious woman for 26+ years and wouldn't trade her for anything. I have been a Christian by Scriptural definition for 35 years and an ordained Deacon for almost 25 years. By Denominational affiliation: Southern Baptist.

About 3-4 weeks ago I found the *PrayerFoundation* ™ website and started reading. I also looked at several other New Monastic community websites. These included Lindisfarne, Iona, Northumbria, Taizé, L'Abri, Jesus Abbey, and several other websites I cannot recall at the moment.

It appears that New Monasticism has the potential to do much good for the Church as a whole. Having examined all of these, you are the only group I would consider joining with.

Your beliefs, as stated, are consistent with my own. Your purpose is timely, and much needed in the Church today. Bible study and prayer are probably the most difficult disciplines to be able consistently to maintain.

Yours in Christ, -Steve (Missouri)

As a teacher I am involved in a project about Peter and Paul in Rome, and of course their persecution. I was therefore really surprised to read about the film *Peter and Paul* that you reviewed on your website.

Dankje wel voor de informatie. Met vriendlijke groet,

-Rob Van V. (Netherlands)

---

*"If we love the Lord Jesus Christ
the burden of our hearts will be
that God may bring us closer together,
so that we may love one another
and rise above all party feeling."*

-Dwight Moody (1837-1899) World Evangelist
Author: *Prevailing Prayer*

126

5.8 Great Lives of Prayer: Thoughts

*"Only a life of prayer and meditation
will render a vessel ready for the Master's use."*

-George Müller (1805-1898)

----

*"We are a body knit together...by a common religious profession,
by unity of discipline, and by the bond of a common hope.
We meet together as an assembly and congregation,
that, offering up prayer to God with united force,
we may wrestle with Him in our supplications."*

-Tertullian (c. 155-c. 220 A.D.)

----

*"A time is coming when men will go mad, and when they see
someone who is not mad, they will attack him saying,
'You are mad -- you are not like us.'"*

-St. Anthony of Egypt (251-356 A.D.)

----

*"There are those who seek knowledge for the sake of knowledge
- that is curiosity.*

*There are those who seek knowledge to be known by others,
- that is vanity.*

*There are those who seek knowledge in order to serve
- that is love."*

-St. Bernard of Clairvaux (1090-1153 A.D.)

----

*"Happiness can only be achieved by looking inward
and learning to enjoy whatever life has,
and this requires transforming greed into gratitude."*

-St. John Chrysostom (c. 347-407 A.D.)

* * *

5.9 Lay Monk Thoughts: Joy

"You will show me the path of life;
in Your presence is fullness of joy."

-Psalm 16:11

Happiness comes and goes. Godly joy remains, another fruit of the Spirit. We received access to this joy as a gift of God's grace, with the indwelling of the Holy Spirit, when we received Christ:

"This is the day that the LORD has made;
we will rejoice and be glad in it!"

-Psalm 118:24

"Nehemiah said, 'Go and enjoy choice food and sweet drinks,
and send some to those who have nothing prepared.

This day is holy to our LORD.
Do not grieve, for the joy of the LORD is your strength.'"

-Nehemiah 8:10

We are always *in God's presence*, because He is always and everywhere present. As Christians, God is always *present within us* through the Holy Spirit. Because of this, we have become a temple of God, and can now live in a continual state of prayer. Our outward circumstances may change, but God does not:

*"Though the fig tree does not bud and there are no grapes on the vines, though the olive crop fails and the fields produce no food, though there are no sheep in the pen and no cattle in the stalls, yet **I will rejoice in the LORD, I will be joyful in God my Savior.***

The Sovereign LORD is my strength;
He makes my feet like the feet of a deer;
He enables me to tread on the heights."

-Habakkuk 3:17-19

* * *

128

S.G. Preston

Brief History of Protestant Monasticism

Protestant Monks? Maybe.

Although he was not aware of it at the time, on Oct. 31, 1517, when Martin Luther nailed his 95 Theses to the door of Wittenburg Cathedral, he began the Protestant Reformation, and some would say, therefore became the first Protestant Monk (Luther was an Augustinian Monk).

Some argue that there were even "pre-Protestant Reformation" Protestant Monks.

In this view, these would include Christians like Francis of Assisi, Thomas á Kempis (Brethren of the Common Life), and with an even stronger case, John Wycliffe's *Lollard* Order of preachers ("The Poor Priests"). Wycliffe taught all of the teachings of the Protestant Reformation in the 1300's: *200 years before Martin Luther*.

Paul D.J. Arblaster, in his book, *"Celtic Christianity Yesterday, Today, and for the Future: Gleaning Wisdom from the Primitive Protestants,"* also makes this case for the Celtic Christian monastics.

Note: Read about Brother Paul and his ministry of evangelism (and an excerpt from his book) in *Brother Paul in the U.K* in Section 8.1 of my book: *Prayer as a Celtic Lay Monk: Learning from Celtic Christian Prayer*.

On the other hand, since Luther ended the monasteries for Protestants, others would not count *any* of these as *Protestant Monks*.

Protestant Monks? Definitely!

1841-42: Anglicans (England, U.S.A., Canada)

In 1841 an Anglican women's monastic community was founded in England.

In 1842 Anglicans created the first practicing Protestant Monks since the dissolution of the monasteries by Henry VIII (300 years earlier), with the founding of the women's *Nashotah Community* in Wisconsin.

This was followed by many others in the U.S.A., Canada, and England, including many other women's Orders.

As of 1990, there were 168 Anglican religious Orders (both men's and women's) throughout the world.

1935: Dietrich Bonhoeffer and a *"New Monasticism"* (Germany)

"...the restoration of the church
will surely come only from
a new type of monasticism
which has nothing in common with the old
but a complete lack of compromise in a life
lived in accordance with
the Sermon on the Mount
in the discipleship of Christ.

I think it is time to gather people together to do this..."

-Dietrich Bonhoeffer (January 14, 1935)

April 26, 1935: Dietrich Bonhoeffer founded a Seminary to train Pastors for the underground *Confessing Church* (Evangelical Christians who were being persecuted by the Nazis).

He was putting into practice his teachings of a *New Monasticism*.

In 1937, Heinrich Himmler declared the Seminary to be illegal, and ordered State Security Police to close it down.

By the following November, 27 of its former students had been arrested. That same year, Dietrich wrote his most famous book: *The Cost of Discipleship*.

Dietrich was executed by the Nazis on Apr. 9, 1945 at Flossenburg Prison, just a few weeks before the end of WWII. He was 39 years old. When the Nazis heard the Allies approaching, they executed all of their prisoners before fleeing. This was standard Nazi policy.

The only reason *anyone* in the camps survived, is because the Nazis didn't have enough time to kill every prisoner, before the Allied Troops could arrive to liberate them.

1946: *Taizé* Community (France)

After WWII, Brother Roger (1915-2001) founded an Independent, International Protestant Religious Order known as Taizé, in France.

Taizé began accepting Eastern Orthodox and Roman Catholics as monks in their Order, as well as those of Protestant background. Brother Roger remained a Protestant Monk his entire life. They now call themselves an Ecumenical Monastic Community.

Note: We are an Evangelical Protestant Lay Monastic Order of *"Mere Christianity"* that also accepts Eastern Orthodox and Roman Catholic Christians as *Oblates*: Lay Monks.

Brother Roger died in 2005 at the age of 90, murdered in Church during an Evening Prayer Service by a mentally ill woman who stabbed him to death with a knife.

1947: *The Evangelical Sisterhood of Mary* (Germany)

In 1947, religious leader and Christian Author, M. Basilea Schlink (1904-2001) Co-founded a Protestant Order for women (with Mother Martyria) in Darmstadt, Germany: *The Evangelical Sisterhood of Mary.*

The founders and first seven sisters became nuns in 1948. The Order currently has 11 Convents located all over the world, with a total of 209 sisters, 130 residing in Darmstadt. Mother Basilea led the Order from 1947 until she went home to be with the Lord in 2001.

1964: *Jesus Abbey* (South Korea)

In 1964, Reuben Archer Torrey III (1918-2002), an Anglican Priest and Missionary in Asia (he had been raised in China, his parents were also missionaries), and his wife, Jane, founded the Jesus Abbey community in South Korea.

Reuben was the grandson of Dwight Moody's fellow servant of the Lord, R.A. Torrey.

After Moody's sudden, unexpected death, Torrey took over his ministry of worldwide evangelism.

Jesus Abbey was begun originally loosely affiliated with the Episcopal Church. They are very Evangelical and sound in Doctrine.

They seem *in actuality* to be a Lay Monastic community, but they do not call themselves that, or use the term "lay monks" in referring to themselves.

1960's-1990's: Lutherans (Monasticism Comes Full Circle)

During this period, a Lutheran Monastery was founded in Denmark, and another in the State of Michigan in the U.S.A.

The *New Monasticism* Movement

1998: *The Simple Way* Community (Philadelphia, Pennsylvania)

Shane Claiborne founds *The Simple Way* Community.

1999: *The Prayer Foundation / Knights of Prayer Lay Monastic Order* ™ (Portland, Oregon / Vancouver, Washington)

Myself, S.G. Preston, and my wife Linda, co-founded *The PrayerFoundation / Knights of Prayer Lay Monastic Order,*™ a *"Mere Christianity"* Interdenominational *"Prayer Encouragement"* ministry, of *"Prayer Teaching and Resources from All Christian Communions and Eras."*

We would not learn of the term *"New Monasticism"* until several years later. Ours was the first Evangelical Monastic Order on the Internet in 1999, and only one for the next four years.

A 1,300 webpage Site, equivalent to twenty 200-page books, receiving up to 2.4 million page downloads per month: 1/2 to 3/4 *billion* total page-views by 2020. Christians from 47 Countries Registered as Lay Monks, and 2,000 more as Prayer Warriors. We have received Prayer requests from 88 Countries.

From the beginning one out of seven of the Lay Monks were either Pastors, Youth Pastors, Missionaries, Bible College, or Seminary students, and this has remained consistent throughout the history of our ministry.

Our definition of a *Lay Monk* is simply:

*"A Christian especially dedicated
to the word of God and prayer."*

-Based on Acts 6:4

2001: Founding of the First Methodist Monastery (Minnesota)

A Methodist Monastery for women was founded in Minnesota: *St. Brigid of Kildare Monastery*.

2002-2003 Communion of Evangelical Episcopal Churches

During 2002-2003, a few Monastic Orders were formed as affiliated Orders of the CEEC (*Communion of Evangelical Episcopal Churches*).

This group, founded in 1995, came out of the *Episcopal Church U.S.A.*, and consisted of Evangelical Episcopal Priests and Congregations.

2003: Rutba House Founded (North Carolina)

Jonathan Wilson-Hartgrove and his wife, Leah, founded the *Rutba House* in North Carolina.

2008: *The Boston Globe* Articles on the *"New Monasticism"* Movement

By 2008 there were over 100 groups describing themselves as both "Evangelical" and "Monastic" in North America alone, according to *The Boston Globe articles: "The unexpected monks..."* and *"In the beginning..."* by Molly Worthen (Feb. 3, 2008).

There are now thousands of such groups worldwide.

Note: These two articles are posted on *The Boston Globe* website and also on our new (2020) website (www.prayerfoundation.net) under the *About Us* Category in the Navigation Bar Menu.

* * *

Brother Paul & Carol: Evangelists in the U.K.

Glastonbury Chaplain / Welsh Coast / Harp CDs / Book

Lay Monk Danny: God's Musician

Original Monastery / Columbia River - Portland, Oregon / CD

Lay Monk Bob: Street Preacher of God

Lay Monk Preston & Lay Monk Linda

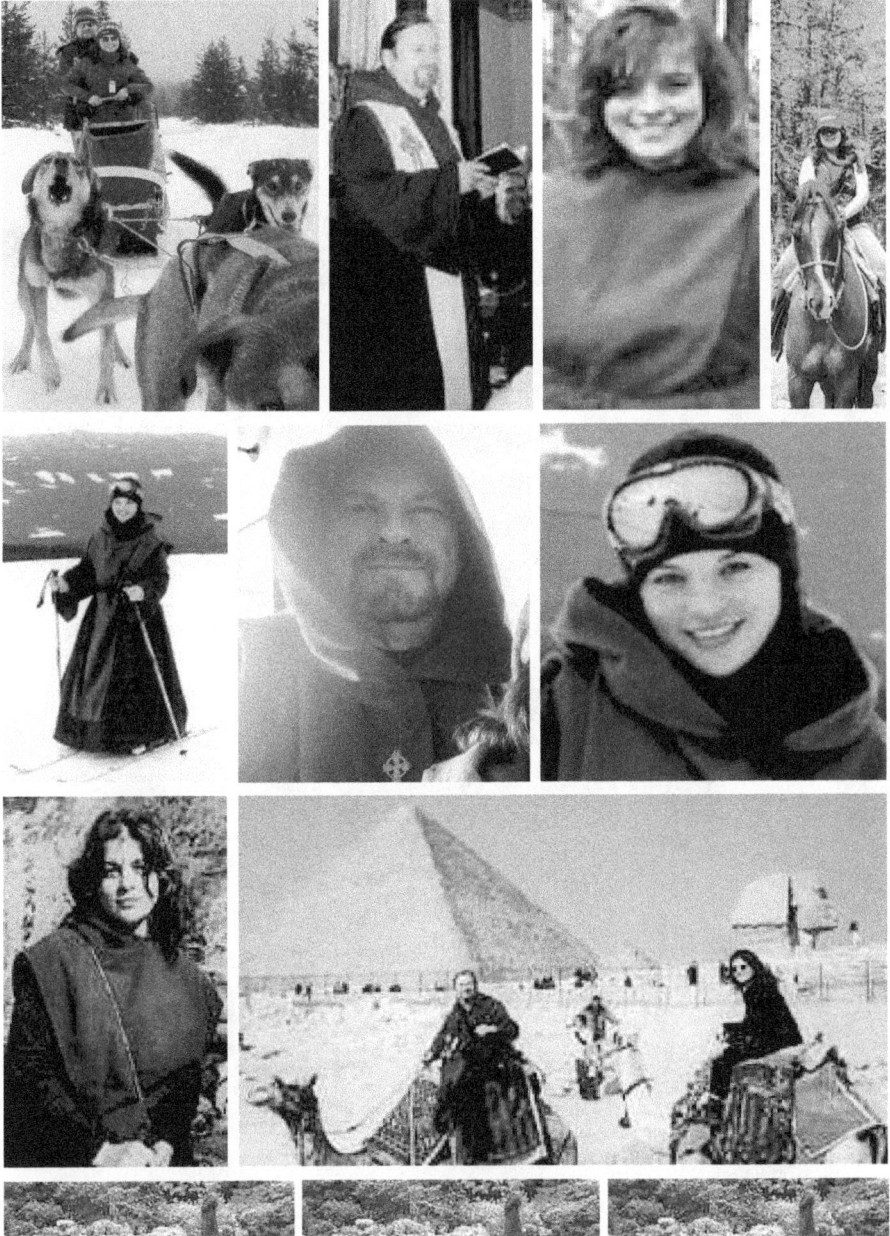

Dogsledding, Wedding, Riding, Skiing, Greece, Egypt

Monk-Dogs, Monk-Cats, & Books

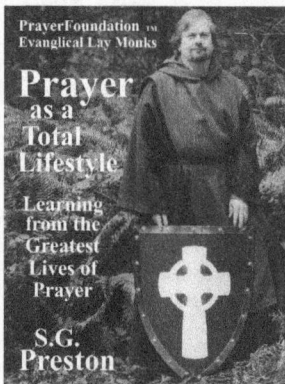

Wolfgang, Batman, Baklava, Barbaro, Baby Blue, & Hermiston

6. *The LORD That Heals* (*Yahweh Rapha*)

6.1 Answer in One Day, Hired in Kuwait, Throat Growth Benign

*"To pray is nothing more involved
than to let Jesus into our needs.*

*To pray is to give Jesus permission
to employ His powers in the alleviation
of our distress.*

*To pray is to let Jesus glorify His Name
in the midst of our needs."*

-O. Hallesby (1879-1961)
Norwegian Lutheran Pastor
Author of the book: *Prayer*

———

*"Rejoicing in hope; patient in tribulation;
continuing constantly in prayer."*

-Romans 12:12

Dec. 7, 2004 - Answer to Prayer:

Praise the Lord!! God answered my prayer and I am getting paid for my work!! Praise God!! Thank you so much for praying! Also, my son's mouth healed nicely from the wisdom teeth extractions. Praise God again! Thank you so much, I know without your prayers, none of this would be positive. God bless each of you, and I pray that God will open many doors for you, filled with lots of blessings.

Love, -Jane (California)

"God hold us to that which drew us first, when the cross was the attraction, and we wanted nothing else."

-Amy Carmichael (1867-1951)
Irish Missionary to India

Dec. 8, 2004 - Answer to Prayer:

I visited Kuwait last week for an interview with my head office management, and they have asked me to join them by January, 2005. Thank you so much also, for praying for delivering me from the negative thoughts / erratic health problems...now I have started to rejoice in my Lord, my Saviour.

Glory be to the Father, and to the Son, and to the Holy Spirit.
-Reema (India)

Dec. 12, 2004 - Answer to Prayer:

Dear fellow Lay Monks, I just wanted to praise the Lord for his provision. My tuition for Spring 2005 is being paid for by the National Guard. I am using my last benefit from the G.I. bill, and I will be a work study at the V.A. hospital near the school.

I will be taking 18 Credit Hours, to complete my requirements for my English Major and Asian Studies Minor, and have already completed enough requirements for a non-teaching Minor in Secondary Education.

Oh, by the way, when I graduate, I hope to apply for the JET program, or help one of my Christian Chinese friends in *****, in teaching English. Depends on financial ability, and the Lord's blessings.

Sincerely, -Lay Monk Stephen (Tennessee)

Feb. 25, 2005 - Answer to Prayer:

I would like to extend my sincerest thanks and love to God the Father for answering my prayers...I am now a fully pledged Medical Doctor, and I owe everything to the Lord our God...*God Is Truly Great!* May this short letter inspire other people to call on God and *Trust His Love.* A *"Thank you very much,"* to the Lay Monks, and others who prayed for me.

God bless all of you. Love, -Michelle

Mar. 3, 2005 - Prayer Request:

I won $1,600.00 for being top in sales in my company: meeting a months-long sales quota over about 120 other sales people. Now my Supervisor and *his* Boss, are trying to find ways to disqualify me, so that I don't receive it. Please pray for God's help in this matter.

Also, please pray that my yellow car will sell, and quickly -- it is very important -- I need the money very badly, and it is a very specialized car, and very difficult to sell.

-Robert (Battleground, Washington)

Mar. 4, 2005 - Answer to Prayer (One Day Later.)

God has answered both prayer requests in one day! My prayer request was posted on the evening of March 3, and the next day my company changed its mind, and stopped trying to disqualify me from receiving the $1,600.00 prize that I had won.

The same day, March 4, the special yellow car that I had been trying to sell for months, because I needed the money so badly, sold!

-Robert (Battleground, Washington)

Mar. 18, 2005 - Answer to Prayer:

Thank you for your prayers! I have been certified to teach Pre-School! Sincerely, -Bonnie

---

May 4, 2005 - Answer to Prayer:

Bless God, Bless God, Bless God!!! A few weeks ago, I asked for prayer for our friend Laurel, who was scheduled for throat surgery on the 20th of April. After surgery, the biopsy showed the growth to be benign, no Cancer, and was diagnosed as a "multi-nodular goiter." She was released from the hospital the next morning! She is recovering nicely and will need medication for only a few months, instead of for life.

God is so faithful! -Doug & Denise (Canada)

May 11, 2005 - Answer to Prayer:

Shalom all...I've sent before two emails from me...requesting for prayers. And I just want to let you all know that the prayers are answered. Praise the *Lord* for all who prayed...thank you so much.

In Christ always, -Siti (Malaysia)

Praise the LORD!
Praise the name of the LORD;
praise Him, you servants of the LORD.

You who stand in the House of the LORD,
in the courtyards of the House of our God;
praise the LORD, for the LORD is good.

Sing praise to His name, for it is pleasant.

The LORD has chosen Jacob for Himself;
Israel for His unique treasure.

I know that the LORD is great,
and that our LORD is above all gods.

Whatever the LORD pleased; that is what He did in heaven,
and on earth, in the seas, and all deep places.

He causes the vapors to ascend, even to the very ends of the earth.
He makes lightning for the rain.
He sends the winds from their storehouses.

He struck the firstborn of Egypt, both of people and of animals.
He sent signs and wonders into the midst of Egypt;
on Pharaoh, and on all of his servants.

God struck great nations and slew mighty kings:
Sihon, king of the Amorites, and Og, king of Bashan,
along with all of the kingdoms of Canaan.

He gave their lands as an inheritance;
an inheritance to Israel, His people.

-Psalm 135:1-12

142

6.2 Low Chances: Healed, Daughter & Little Boy Found

"God shapes the world by prayer.

The more prayer there is in the world
the better the world will be,
the mightier the forces
against evil..."

-E.M. Bounds (1835-1913) Methodist Minister
Author*: Power Through Prayer*

———

"Continue in prayer; and be watchful,
with thanksgiving."

-Colossians 4:2

May 12, 2005 - Answer to Prayer:

I hope you are receiving God's abundant blessings already poured out on you. A thousand thanks for your prayers. For Patrick, who was released from the hospital Monday, after eight hours of surgery Friday.

For his father Don, who has come to life, and seems like another man. For Kyle, who is fine. For yours truly, who is swimming through what seems to be molasses in so many areas, but especially the emotional area.

Grace and Peace in Christ, -Ken

P.S., I quit a job that had become an emotional burden, the day I got what was supposed to be my *second* job.

I have received two scriptural exhortations from my new manager this week, who *"just happens"* to be a Pastor who is planting a church.

Gloria A Dios! A Su Nombre! Gloria!

May 15, 2005 - Answer to Prayer:

Praise the Lord Jesus Christ, Alleluia. Many thanks to you for all the fervent prayers you have offered up to the Almighty God on behalf of me and my family. The Almighty God has been very gracious to me, and in His mercy, He has been healing me, and delivering me supernaturally. I am very happy to tell you, that the Almighty God has delivered me totally from the severe pain I was getting in my back, from my neck downwards.

The bugs that were troubling us are no more to be seen. My niece has passed the 3rd standard with flying colours. Mr. A.'s house has been sold finally, and he is very happy. Lily's husband has finally got another job abroad, and he will be staying there. Lily's daughter is healed of all infections she had in her blood. Mr. K. has been promoted.

Well, this is all for now. May the Almighty God shower his abundant blessings upon you and your ministry. May he richly reward you for your faithfulness in interceding for me and my family, and for all those whom I requested you to pray for.

Yours in Christ always, -Sandra (India)

June 21, 2005 - Answer to Prayer:

I had asked before, for prayer for my dear friend Jim. Since that time, he did manage to find a home, is no longer homeless, and has been working so hard to make a good life for his four children. He has started reading the Bible and praying, and things have really been looking up for him. Blessings to you, -Karen

---

"Men who know their God are before anything else men who pray, and the first point where their zeal and energy for God's glory come to expression is in their prayers. If there is little energy for such prayer, and little consequent practice of it, this is a sure sign that as yet we scarcely know our God."

-J.I. Packer (1926-2020)
Author: *Knowing God*

144

June 27, 2005 - Answer to Prayer:

Thanks! The prayer request we made a while ago, was for a co-worker's father (Mr. D.), who was in Critical Condition with internal bleeding for several weeks.

Doctors gave him almost no chance to survive. He has now checked out of the Hospital in Normal Condition -- the Doctors were very surprised at his unexpected recovery, when the chances were so low.

-Robert (Washington State)

July 15, 2005 - Prayer Request:

Dear fellow Lay Monks, My cousin's daughter has a missing daughter that was abducted. Her name is *****. She is fifteen years old. The details are rather horrific to mention, so please pray for her safety, and for the Holy Spirit to convict the man of his wrongdoing. I think she will be added to *Operation Look Out* in a short time.

Sincerely, -Lay Monk Stephen (Tennessee)

Answer to Prayer - July 16, 2005 (One Day Later.)

Dear fellow Lay Monks, Thank you for your prayers. ***** has been located in Denver, Colorado. I don't know much on details, but at least she is alive and found.

Sincerely, -Lay Monk Stephen (Tennessee)

July 27, 2005 - Prayer Request:

Dear *Prayer Warriors*, my sister sent me this and it made me cry -- people are emailing this little boy's photo to as many people as they can, to try and find his relatives. Please pray that this comes true. Kind regards, -Bernadette

Answer to Prayer - July 27, 2005 (The Same Day.)

Dear *Prayer Warriors*, I have just found out he is O.K., and now with family...you certainly do have prayers answered quickly, don't you!!! Kindly, -Bernadette

---

Aug. 5, 2005 - Answer to Prayer:

Praise God for His faithfulness! A short time ago, I asked you to pray for our friend Gord, who had been suddenly and unexpectedly released from his long term job with a Christian Service agency. I just learned today, that he has signed a one-year management contract with a ministry that works with folks leaving prison.

This is very much in his heart, and it will allow him more time in direct contact with the people he helps. Our thanks to our fellow *Prayer Warriors* around the world, for your faithfulness in prayer.

-Brother Seamus (Ontario, Canada)

**Your name, O LORD, endures forever,
along with Your memorial, O LORD,
throughout all generations.**

The LORD will judge his people:
and concerning His servants, He shall be comforted.

The idols of the pagan nations are silver and gold,
the work of men's hands.

They have mouths, but they do not speak;
they have eyes, but they do not see.

They have ears, but they do not hear.
There is no breath in their mouths.

Those who make them are like them,
and so is everyone who trusts in them.

Praise the LORD, descendants of Israel;
praise the LORD, descendants of Aaron.

**Praise the LORD, descendants of Levi;
you who reverence the LORD, praise the LORD.**

Praised be the LORD from Zion,
for He dwells in Jerusalem.
Praise the LORD!

-Psalm 135:13-21

6.3 Much Improved, India Christians Not Killed, Many Blessings

"All our strength lies in prayer!"

-Charles Spurgeon (1834-1892)
Author: *The Treasury of David*
(Commentary on the Psalms)

———

"Then shall you call upon Me,
'and you shall go
and pray to Me,
and I will hear you."

-Jeremiah 29:12

Aug. 24, 2005 - Prayer Request:

Please pray for complete healing for my mother-in-law, Marilyn, who has Pancreatic Cancer and Gall Bladder problems. She had been recovering with your prayers; the Cancer shrinking, when she had a Gall Bladder attack.

They need to operate on this first, but cannot because her weight is too low (95 lbs.) due to the Chemotherapy. She also has an additional problem that makes it very difficult for her to gain weight.

-Annette (Goldendale, Washington)

Answer to Prayer - Sept. 20, 2005 (Twenty-seven Days Later.)

The Lord healed my mother-in-law Marilyn's problem that was preventing the weight gain, so they were able to have a Gall Bladder operation, which also went successfully.

The Pancreatic Cancer has been shrinking for months now; since you have been praying for her; and is now down to the size of a walnut, and not spreading.

-Annette (Goldendale, Washington)

Oct. 10, 2005 - Answer to Prayer:

Blessings all!!! During the summer I asked you to pray for my cousin, who was in the midst of a difficult pregnancy. I am *delighted!!!* to report that on Monday she delivered a beautiful 8 pound, 4 ounce baby girl! Both are doing well, and they are expected home in the next few days.

-Brother Seamus (Ontario, Canada)

Nov. 18, 2005 - Prayer Request:

Please pray for the believers in the Himachal Pradesh region of India. A group of radical Hindus have beaten a Pastor, and threatened to burn more than 60 new converts to death if they do not re-convert to Hinduism.

This area is home to a large shrine to the Hindu "god" Shiva, and since the tourist visits are so important to the local economy, the police are dragging their feet in becoming involved. Please pray for the protection of the believers, and pray that the hearts of the attackers would be softened to the Gospel.

Thank you again for praying, -Brother Seamus (Ontario, Canada)

Answer to Prayer (Two Days Later.) Received Nov. 27, 2005

Bless God! The plan to kill believers in Himachal Pradesh (India) if they did not reconvert to Hinduism has been thwarted. The date set was Sunday the 20th of November. The only ceremony that day was *church!*

And the police, who had been trying to stay uninvolved, actually met with the Hindu community (including the media!) and explained that Christian conversion was one of choice, and that the new believers had not been coerced.

They told the people that those who had been speaking against the church were misleading them. The Pastor's son said that they met without incident.

-Brother Seamus (Ontario, Canada)

148

S.G. Preston

Jan. 2, 2006 – Answer to Prayer:

We thank and praise the Lord and Saviour, Jesus Christ, for his *overflow* of blessings on our family this past year…2005, in the form of:

1) My Job Promotion. 2) Baby. 3) New Job. 4) New House.

5) Lots of other blessings.

We thank you, your ministry: for your fervent prayers and blessings on our family. We will pray for your Ministry that this coming year…2006, be filled with surprise blessings, and end-time intensified anointing upon your ministry, loved ones, and partners.

Please do pray for us too...upon our family, and that in the new house, I should start a Care-cell Ministry. We conclude by wishing you and yours: *A Very Happy, Prosperous and Blessed New Year - 2006!!!* Thanking You. Sincerely Yours,

-Anand, wife Jerline, and baby Evelyn (Madras, India)

Jan. 4, 2006 - Answer to Prayer:

Thank you for your prayers, as my nephew is now married, after a long search for a suitable bride. Once again: many, many thanks for your timely prayers.

Yours gratefully, -Philomena

Jan. 23, 2006 - Answer to Prayer:

Praise the Lord! JoAnn and Stephanie went to church with us today (what a blessing the service was for us), and Joanne brought another friend with her. They all say they are going to go from now on; they love the church.

The Lord's done so much for us, *Praise His Holy Name!* Thank you so much. God bless.

Love, -Jane (California)

Jan. 25, 2006 - Prayer Request:

Please pray for a lady named Andi, who is going into surgery. Pray that they not find any Cancer or anything else serious.

-Robert (Washington State)

Answer to Prayer: Jan. 28, 2006 (Three Days Later.)

Andi had the surgery, and everything is fine! No Cancer or other problems were found!

Thank you for praying, -Robert (Washington State)

A Psalm of David.

I will praise You with my whole heart;
before the angels, I will sing praise to You.
I will worship toward Your holy Temple,
and praise Your name for Your loving kindness
and Your truth.

For You have exalted Your word and Your name above all.
On the day that I cried out, You answered me,
and strengthened me in my soul.

All the kings of the earth shall praise You, O LORD,
when they hear the words from Your mouth.
Yes, they shall sing in the ways of the LORD,
for great is the glory of the LORD.

Though the LORD is on high,
yet He has regard for the lowly;
but He distances Himself from the proud.

Though I walk in the midst of trouble, You will revive me.
You shall stretch out Your hand against the wrath of my enemies,
and Your right hand shall rescue me.

The LORD will complete what He has begun in me.
Your mercy, O LORD, endures forever;
do not abandon those who are the work of Your own hands.

-Psalm 138

150

6.4 Lay Monk Bob Healed, Job in India, Pardon in Samoa

*"Prayer is not overcoming
God's reluctance,
but laying hold of
His willingness."*

-Martin Luther (1483-1546)

———

*"Now when Daniel knew
that the writing was signed,
he went into his house;
and his windows being opened
in his chamber
toward Jerusalem,
he kneeled upon his knees
three times a day,
and prayed,
and gave thanks before his God,
as he had done before."*

-Daniel 6:10

Mar. 22, 2006 - Prayer Request:

Please pray for our own Lay Monk Bob, who recently began suffering from much low back pain problems, due to the delayed effect of an injury received many years ago.

-The Lay Monks (Vancouver, Washington)

Answer to Prayer: Mar. 28, 2006 (Six Days Later.)

Thank you so much for praying; now give thanks with us to God. Lay Monk Bob's back is no longer bothering him!

-The Lay Monks (Vancouver, Washington)

Mar. 23, 2006 - Prayer Request:

Could you pray for my uncle; who is going through a terrible time with a lost job. Please pray for the Lord's guidance, and that he gets another job.

-Vijay (India)

Answer to Prayer: Apr. 17, 2006 (Seven Weeks Later.)

Dear beloved, I thank you and your ministry for your love, prayers and support. My uncle's got a job!

Thanking you once again. In Him, -Vijay (India)

June 2, 2006 - Answer to Prayer:

The Doctor tested Matt's tissue under the Melanoma, and the Cancer was only in the epidermis (skin). His prognosis is very good; no Chemo or anything required. Next week they are checking the cells to be sure they are still clear.

Thank you for praying. -Donna (Massachusetts)

July 7, 2006 - Answer to Prayer:

Dear Prayer Warriors, Praise our wonderful, wonderful, Lord Jesus Christ! I requested prayers for my husband, who is Chieftain of his Clan. He was banned from village, because he stood up for one of village youths involved in brawl.

The youth was fined a very ridiculous amount. There was no way he could possibly pay fine. Much of village laws still practiced, belongs to dark ages.

My husband preached Jesus into the Council Meeting in way of reforming some of these laws.

Has made many enemies since involved in village affairs. However, your prayers were answered, and even though he did not agree to the penalty, and ban, but he obeyed the law.

He rounded up his family, and raised the amount for the fine.

152

On delivering it, the council were emotional, and thanked him for his godly wisdom, and pardoned all the Chiefs, totaling six, who had also been banned from village.

Some had been out for several years, but because of my husband, they received pardon. It was truly an emotional time. Praise, glory, and honour, be returned to our heavenly Father!

Thank you for your faithful service for our Lord Jesus Christ!

-Tifi (Samoa)

July 15, 2006 - Answer to Prayer:

Praise God, my Hepatitis C viral level is *undetectable!* After only three months of the one year of treatment; plus no signs of anemia! ....And as an *extra* Heavenly bonus -- my HIV viral level is *also* undetectable.

God Is Good!!! Thank you, Jesus!

In the past, I had very high viral levels; i.e. my Hepatitis C as high as 19 million; I also had bad past reactions to liver treatment, getting severe anemia, and having to be hospitalized two times last year for emergency blood transfusions.

Most people get many side effects from these weekly injections, but this time I am doing very well. Thank you.

Jesus Is The Great Physician! -Ricardo (Brooklyn, New York)

Aug. 11, 2006 - Answer to Prayer:

I have already lost 20 pounds, and have indeed been approved for SSI disability, which a Judge has okayed. Now I can take care of my senior mom so she can retire! We are also in a church every Sunday, and love what God is doing, as we are in His perfect will!

I am a Believer, and I still struggle with a mental illness known as O.C.D., and am waiting on the Lord to heal me of so much anxiety!

-Thanks for your prayers, and be blessed.

Sept. 20, 2006 - Answer to Prayer:

Nancy called, and she and her husband are working out their problems. Thank you so much for praying. She is truly grateful for all prayers.

-Jane (California)

Sept. 27, 2006 -Answer to Prayer:

Dear beloved, thank you for praying for my grandmother. She is much, much better.

In Him, -Vijay (India)

**By the rivers of Babylon; there we sat down.
Yes, we wept, when we remembered Zion.**

We hung our harps upon the willows in its midst.
But the wicked who carried us away to captivity,
required from us a song.

Those who tormented us, demanded mirth from us, saying,
"Sing us one of the songs of Zion."
How shall we sing the LORD's song in a strange land?

If I forget you, O Jerusalem, let my right hand forget its cunning.
If I do not remember you, let my tongue cling to the roof of my
mouth; if I do not prefer Jerusalem above my chief joy.

-Psalm 137:1-6

---

*"If we truly think of Christ as our source of holiness,
we shall refrain from anything wicked or impure in thought or act,
and thus show ourselves to be worthy bearers of His name.*

*For the quality of holiness is shown not by what we say,
but by what we do."*

-St. Gregory of Nyssa (c. 335-c. 395 A.D.)

154

6.5 *Prayer Warrior* Comments

Dear Brothers and Sisters in Christ, I am writing to tell you that your website is helping to change my life. I was raised in the Church and have been a Christian for many years, but I was a lazy Christian.

I rarely read the Bible, quit going to Church because it became too political, and generally only prayed when I wanted something.

Recently, I've started praying for the *Prayer Requests* that come in on the *Prayerchain* and I feel that my prayers are being heard and making a difference.

My prayer has become so much more than it was before, and I feel like I'm actually making a connection with God now.

I've read more of the Bible in the last four weeks than I've read in the last four years, and I truly believe the Holy Spirit is guiding me. My main purpose in writing is to ask to become a Lay Monk with the *PrayerFoundation.*™

I want to thank you for such a great ministry. I have found so many resources on your website, and I really feel like I'm growing in my walk with Christ. I'm going to start directing others to your Site. Thank you again for all that you do.

In Christ, -James G. (Florida)

Dear friends in Jesus! I am so excited because I have found some who are willing to pray for me and our Sunday Schools in Nordmore. I have already read your reply many times. This is my first day after the Holidays. God bless you and thanks a lot.

-Hans O., *Sunday School Minister* (Norway)

"The more you praise, the more vigor you will have for prayer; and the more you pray, the more matter you will have for praise."

-J.I. Packer (1926-2020)
Author: *Knowing God*

6.6 Prayer & Church Government

"Are any sick among you?
Let them call for the elders of the church,
and let the elders pray over them,
anointing them with oil
in the name of the Lord:

And the prayer of faith shall deliver the sick,
and the Lord shall raise them up;
and if they have committed sins,
they shall be forgiven them.

Confess your faults to one another,
and pray for one another,
that you may be healed.

The effectual fervent prayer
of a righteous person
has much power."

-James 5:14-16

Some Types of Church Government In Use Today

1. *Episcopal:* Bishop, Priests / Ministers, Deacons (Hierarchical Authority).

2. *Presbyterian:* Representative Democracy (Congregation elects Presbyters / Elders / Board of Directors).

3. *Pure Democracy:* Congregation votes on everything, based on *"the priesthood of all believers"* (Baptists).

4. *Consensus:* Unanimous agreement required before any action is taken (Quakers / Religious Society of Friends).

"God answers the prayer we ought to have made
rather than the prayer we did make."

-J.I. Packer (1926-2020)

Freedom In Christ

Church government in the New Testament experienced several changes within only the first fifty years of the completion of the New Testament, apparently in response to the tremendous growth in numbers of Christians.

It seems to have been regarded by the Early Church as an area not where a particular form was solely authorized or commanded, but instead where the Christian's *"freedom in Christ"* (subject to the leading of the Holy Spirit) was applicable.

As Dr. J. Vernon McGee (1904-1988; *Thru the Bible* radio ministry) so accurately points out, what is truly important is the quality, spirituality, and doctrinal soundness of the individual Christians involved.

That *all* of the various types of church government "work" when good, spiritual, Biblically sound Christians are involved -- and that *none of them* "work" when the opposite is true.

The Lord's Prayer

"Pray then in this way..." -Matthew 6:9
"When you pray, say..." Luke 11:2

———

(The Lord's Prayer is) *"...truly the summary of the whole Gospel."*

-Tertullian (Writing c. 200 A.D.)

———

"If we pray rightly, and as becomes our wants,
we say nothing but what is already contained in the Lord's Prayer."

-St. Augustine (354-430 A.D.)

———

"I am convinced that when a Christian rightly prays The Lord's Prayer...His praying is more than adequate."

-Martin Luther (1483-1546)

157

6.7 Dear *PrayerFoundation* ™

Greetings and a Blessed Easter to you all! I'd signed up as a Prayer Warrior awhile back... The idea of (Lay) Monks really appeals to me and is a powerful balance to the increasing secularization and insanity I see growing in this world.

Also, as an ethnic Celt, I am impressed by, and truly love how you have incorporated Celtic Christianity into your ministry, and how grounded in Scripture and the Faith y'all are. What a blessing your Site is to me!

In His Peace, -Alexis M. (Pelham, Tennessee)

Subscribe me to your Monthly E-Newsletter. Be strong and be humble. In His Peace,

-Brother Joe C.J.+ (Charlotte, North Carolina)

(Survey) *Born-again?* **Yes.**
Visit Site? Weekly.
Age Group? 18-29.
Comments? I was very impressed.
I had some concerns about "religious" beliefs which kill true spirituality, but that didn't last long. :)

-Daniel (South Africa)

I pray for you that your faith does not stop.

God bless you, -Pastor Joh. M. (Berlin, Germany)

"God has spoken to man, and the Bible is His Word, given to us to make us wise unto salvation.... Godliness means responding to God's revelation in trust and obedience, faith and worship, prayer and praise, submission and service. Life must be lived in the light of God's Word. This, and nothing else, is true religion."

-J.I. Packer (1926-2020)

158

S.G. Preston

6.8 Justin Martyr: Early Christian Worship & Persecution

Justin Martyr's "First Apology" (On Christian Worship)

"And He said to them, 'It is written:
My House shall be called the House of Prayer...'"

-Matthew 21:13

———

"We used to hate and destroy one another,
and refuse to associate with people of another race or country.
Now, because of Christ, we live together with all people,
and pray for our enemies."

-Justin Martyr (c. 100-165 A.D.)

He Taught & Defended Christianity

Justin Martyr was born c. 100 A.D., in Flavia Neapolis (today's Nablus, Israel). He converted to Christianity c. 130 A.D. and suffered martyrdom in Rome c. 165 A.D.

Justin Martyr's *First Apology* is the oldest non-New Testament record we have of how early Christian worship (liturgy) was conducted. A Christian Apologist, Justin taught and defended Christianity in Asia Minor and at Rome.

Note: The words *Apologetics, Apology,* and Christian *Apologists,* are not derived from the English word *apologize,* but from the ancient Greek word *apologia* (ἀπολογία - *to give an answer to questions and objections, to justify*).

"In your hearts, set apart Christ as Lord, and be ready always
to give an answer (apologia) to everyone that asks you,
a reason for the hope that is in you, with humility and reverence.

Having a good conscience that,
while they speak evil of you, as evildoers, they may be ashamed,
who falsely accuse your good lifestyle in Christ."

-1 Peter 3:15-16

Excerpts from Justin Martyr's *First Apology* (Written 150 A.D.)

Note: In Chapter 62, it is implied that Christians removed their footwear before worship.

Chapter 65. Administration of the Sacraments

"Having ended the prayers, we salute one another with a kiss. There is then brought to the president of the brethren bread and a cup of wine mixed with water.

He taking them, gives praise and glory to the Father of the universe, through the name of the Son and of the Holy Spirit, and offers thanks at considerable length for our being counted worthy to receive these things at His hands.

When he has concluded the prayers and thanksgivings, all the people present express their assent by saying: *Amen.* This word *Amen* answers in the Hebrew language to the Greek *γEνοιτο* (*so be it*).

When the president has given thanks, and all the people have expressed their assent, those who are called deacons by us give to each of those present to partake of the bread and wine mixed with water.

Over which the thanksgiving was pronounced, and to those who are absent they carry away a portion.

Chapter 67. Weekly Worship of the Christians

We afterwards continually remind each other of these things.

The wealthy among us help the needy; and we always keep together; and for all things with which we are supplied, we bless the Maker of all through His Son Jesus Christ, and through the Holy Spirit.

And on the day called Sunday, all who live in cities or in the country gather together to one place, and the memoirs of the apostles or the writings of the prophets are read, as long as time permits.

Then, when the reader has ceased, the president verbally instructs, and exhorts to the imitation of these good things.

S.G. Preston

All Rise Together & Pray

Then we all rise together and pray, and, as I said before, when our prayer is ended, bread and wine and water are brought. And the president in like manner offers prayers and thanksgivings, according to his ability, and the people assent, saying *Amen*.

There is a distribution to each, and a participation of that over which thanks have been given, and to those who are absent a portion is sent by the deacons.

And they who are well to do, and willing, give what each thinks fit; and what is collected is deposited with the president, who succors the orphans and widows.

And also those who, through sickness or any other cause, are in want, and those who are in bonds, and the strangers sojourning among us; and in a word takes care of all who are in need.

On the First Day

But Sunday is the day on which we all hold our common assembly, because it is the first day on which God, having wrought a change in the darkness and matter, made the world; and Jesus Christ our Savior, on the same day rose from the dead.

For He was crucified on the day before, that of Saturn (Saturday). On the day after that of Saturn, which is the day of the Sun, having appeared to His apostles and disciples, He taught them these things: which we have submitted to you also for your consideration."

———

My Comments On Justin Martyr's Text

*"The world suffers nothing from Christians
but hates them because they reject its pleasures."
"...now we cultivate the reverence of God, justice, kindness, faith,
and the expectation of the future given us
through the Crucified One..."*

-Justin Martyr (c. 100-165 A.D.)

161

Footwear Removed Before Worship

The out-of-doors, homes, and catacombs (underground cemeteries) were used as early places of Christian worship.

During the first 300 years of Christianity, *simply being a Christian* was a capital crime, punishable by death.

After 313 A.D., when the Roman Emperor Constantine declared Christianity legal, dedicated Church buildings came into general use, and footwear was removed before entering.

This practice was observed among Christians at least up through the beginning of the seventh century.

This Early Church practice was retained from the earlier Jewish Temple observance, which was based on the commandment of God to Moses at the burning bush:

> *"And He said,*
> *'Do not draw near;*
> *remove your sandals*
> *from your feet,*
>
> *for the place*
> *on which you stand*
> *is holy ground.'"*

-Exodus 3:5

Giving of *The Peace*

Our modern *Peace*, or *Greeting*. The kiss of peace greeting is still observed in Middle Eastern and European Eastern Orthodox worship services.

Greek was the common vernacular language in use among the people at the time of Justin's writing, even in Rome, and worship services were held using it.

Church officers at this time seem to have consisted of a President (Bishop / Pastor) and Deacons.

S.G. Preston

Order of Worship Service (Liturgy)

The Trinity is invoked: Father, Son, and Holy Spirit.

Reading of God's Word, the Holy Scriptures.

Christian Teaching.

"Then we all rise..." Were all seated during the Homily / Sermon / Christian Teaching?

All rise for standing prayer on Sunday.

As in the New Testament, an offering is taken for the purpose of helping fellow Christians: orphans and widows, the poor and needy, prisoners, and *"...strangers sojourning among us."*

——

Martyrdom of Justin Martyr

*"But since we do not place our hopes
on the present (order),
we are not troubled by being put to death,
since we will have to die somehow in any case."*

*"The more we are persecuted
and martyred,
the more others
in ever increasing numbers
become believers."*

-Justin Martyr (c. 100-165 A.D.) Church Father

What System of Teaching Do You Profess?

"The saints were seized and brought before the Prefect of Rome, whose name was Rusticus. As they stood before the judgment seat, Rusticus the Prefect said to Justin, 'Above all, have faith in the gods and obey the Emperors.'

Justin replied, 'We cannot be accused or condemned for obeying the commands of our Savior, Jesus Christ.'

Rusticus said, 'What system of teaching do you profess?'

You Are a Christian, Then?

Justin said, 'I have tried to learn about every system, but I have accepted the true doctrines of the Christians, though these are not approved by those who are held fast by error.'

The Prefect Rusticus said, 'Are those doctrines approved by you, wretch that you are?'

Justin said, 'Yes, for I follow them with their correct teaching.'

The Prefect Rusticus said, 'What sort of teaching is that?'

Justin said, 'Worship the God of the Christians. We hold Him to be from the beginning the one Creator and Maker of the whole creation, of things seen and things unseen.

We worship also the Lord Jesus Christ, the Son of God.'

Rusticus said, "You are a Christian, then?"

Justin said, 'Yes, I am a Christian.'

Offer Sacrifice to the Gods

The Prefect said to Justin, 'You are called a learned man and think you know what is true teaching. Listen: if you were scourged and beheaded, are you convinced that you would go up to heaven?'

Justin said, 'I hope that I shall enter God's house if I suffer in that way. For I know that God's favor is stored up until the end of the whole world for all who have lived good lives.'

The Prefect Rusticus said, 'Do you have an idea that you will go up to heaven to receive some suitable rewards?"

Justin said, 'It is not an idea that I have; it is something I know well and hold to be most certain.'

The Prefect Rusticus said, 'Now let us come to the point at issue, which is necessary and urgent. Gather round then and with one accord offer sacrifice to the gods.'

Justin said, 'No one who is right-thinking stoops from true worship to false worship.'

S.G. Preston

The Witness of Martyrdom

The Prefect Rusticus said, 'If you do not do as you are commanded you will be tortured without mercy.'

Justin said, 'We hope to suffer torment for the sake of our Lord Jesus Christ, and so be saved.'

In the same way the other martyrs also said, 'Do what you will. We are Christians; we do not offer sacrifice to idols.'

The Prefect Rusticus pronounced sentence, saying, 'Let those who have refused to sacrifice to the gods and to obey the command of the Emperor be scourged and led away to suffer capital punishment according to the ruling of the laws.'

Glorifying God, the holy martyrs were beheaded, and so fulfilled their witness of martyrdom in confessing their faith in their Savior."

-Excerpted from: *Acts of the Martyrdom of Saint Justin and His Companions* (165 A.D.)

The Lord's Prayer

*"He who best knew what we ought to pray for,
and how we ought to pray...*

*As the moral law was written with the finger of God,
so this prayer was dropped from the lips of the Son of God.*

He knew what manner of address would most please Himself...

***He has here dictated to us a most perfect
and universal form of prayer,***
*comprehending all our real wants,
expressing all our lawful desires;*

*a complete directory
and full exercise
of all our devotions."*

-John Wesley (1703-1791)
Founder: *Methodists*

165

6.9 Lay Monk Thoughts: Persecution, Patience & Peace

"Peace I leave with you, My peace I give you; not as the world gives, do I give to you.

Let not your heart be troubled, neither let it be afraid."

-John 14:27

If They Have Persecuted Me, They Will Persecute You (John 16:20)

If you do not want to *offend* anyone:

> You cannot *say* anything.
> You cannot *do* anything.
> You cannot *be* anything.

Especially, *you cannot be a Christian*, for *Christians* are an *offense* to this world that rejects God. The Apostle Paul calls this:

"...the offense of the cross..."

-Galatians 5:11

Your *very existence as a Christian* makes the world think about the God of the Bible, who the world hates.

They hate Him because He is a God of *absolute truth*, a concept that they totally reject. They hate Him because He is a God of *morality*, and this, *His morality*, the world also rejects. Because the people of the world are not willing to give up their sins.

In addition, the world demands that you not only *accept* their grossest sins, but that you declare their worst evils to be *good and right*. And if you do not do this, they will hate and reject you.

The world will be offended and react in anger and hatred, in their intolerance and bigotry; which they deny having, and instead *falsely accuse you*, as Christians, of having.

Persecution, Patience, & Peace

How can we reconcile the persecution from both the world and the evil powers that control it, with the promise of God's peace?

> *"My people will dwell*
> *in peaceful dwelling places,*
> *in secure homes,*
> *in undisturbed places*
> *of rest."*

-Isaiah 32:18 (NIV)

We do so by allowing God's grace, in His gift of patience as a fruit of the Holy Spirit, to flow through us, manifesting God's love in our lives:

> *"And hope does not put us to shame,*
> *because God's love has been*
> *poured out through our hearts*
> *by the Holy Spirit,*
> who has been
> given to us."

-Romans 5:5

As Christians, we live in a temple of God, our bodies indwelt by the Holy Spirit. God is always our refuge in this chaotic, fallen world; this world of persecution:

> *"God is our refuge and strength,*
> *a very present help in trouble.*
>
> *Therefore we will not fear;*
> *though the earth be removed,*
> *and the mountains*
> *be carried*
> *into the midst*
> *of the sea."*

-Psalm 46:1

We Are Called to Walk in Love (Ephesians 5:2)

As Christians we are called to be conformed to Christ: to reject the world and instead manifest Christ's love, kindness, patience, and peace.

"Love is patient and kind..."

-1 Corinthians 13:4

"Yes, all that live godly in Christ Jesus shall suffer persecution."

-2 Timothy 3:12

"...they shall lay their hands upon you and persecute you,
delivering you up to the synagogues, and into prisons,
being brought before kings and rulers for My name's sake.

It will lead to an opportunity to give testimony.
Settle it therefore in your hearts, not to meditate before what you
shall answer; for I will give you words and wisdom,
which all your adversaries will not be able to contradict or resist.

And you shall be betrayed by parents,
brothers and sisters, relatives, and friends;
and some of you they will cause to be put to death...

In your patience you possess your souls."

-Luke 21:12-17, 19

When Pharaoh and his army trapped the children of Israel at the Red Sea, just before God opened a way for the Jewish people to escape, drowning their persecutors:

"Moses said to the people,
'Do not be afraid. Stand still,
and see the salvation of the LORD,
which He will show you today:

These Egyptians that you
now see before you, you shall see
no more again forever."

-Exodus 14:13

168

S.G. Preston

Our Anger Must Be Rejected As Sin

We need our anger to be replaced by Christ's patience and peace.

*"Anger is a perversion of courage,
as lust is a perversion of love."*

-St. Gregory of Nyssa (c. 335-c. 395 A.D.)

Of course, there is a *righteous anger* against evil and injustice in this world:

"Be angry but do not sin."

-Psalm 4:4 in the Greek *Septuagint*,
quoted by Paul in Ephesians 4:26

...but most of our anger is regrettably not of this kind. Instead, it is sin. This is what James is speaking of when he states:

"The wrath of man does not produce the righteousness of God."

-James 1:20

Our problem is that we find attempts to control our anger to be a losing battle:

*"For the good that I want to do, I do not do;
but the evil which I do not want to do, that I do."*

-Romans 7:19

The answer (as always!) is Christ:

"Apart from Me you can do nothing."

-John 15:5

The Peace of God

We must go to God in prayer. The Norwegian Lutheran Pastor O. Hallesby, was a prisoner for two years in a Concentration Camp, for his opposition to the Nazis during World War II.

As he correctly points out, we are indeed helpless. We must *pray for grace* to overcome sin.

169

Brother Lawrence (1614-1691), a Carmelite Monk, also taught this in the book, *The Practice of the Presence of God*:

"In difficulties we need only have recourse to Jesus Christ, and beg His grace, with which everything became easy."

We must *pray for grace* to be *conformed to the image of Christ*. And we have total confidence that God will answer this prayer, because we know that it is His will for us. Scripture assures us:

"For who He did foreknow, He also did predestinate to be conformed to the image of His Son; that He might be the firstborn among many brethren."

-Romans 8:29

———

"Cast all your cares upon Him, for He cares for you."

-1 Peter 5:7

———

"Be filled with care for nothing; but in everything by prayer and supplication with thanksgiving let your requests be made known to God.

And the peace of God, which passes all understanding, shall keep your hearts and minds through Christ Jesus."

-Philippians 4:5-7

———————————————————————————————

"We must learn to measure ourselves, not by our knowledge about God, not by our gifts and responsibilities in the church, but by how we pray and what goes on in our hearts.

Many of us, I suspect, have no idea how impoverished we are at this level. Let us ask the Lord to show us."

-J.I. Packer (1926-2020)

7. *The Everlasting God (El Olam)*

7.1 Samoa Justice, Walking Again, Grandson Out of Hospital

"We must not let any season pass without thanksgiving."

-St. Athanasius of Alexandria
(296/298-373 A.D.)
Author: *On the Incarnation*

———

"The LORD is near to all that call upon Him,
to all that call upon Him in truth."

-Psalm 145:18

Oct. 20, 2006 - Answer to Prayer:

Dear *Prayer Warriors*, God is truth, and so faithful.

Had requested prayers for my husband, and 3-fold ministry: High Chief for family and village, member of Judiciary Commission, and Chaplain for Govt. Prayer House.

Enemy has been trying for past two years, ever since he was called into these roles, to block and destroy him. Wherever God's favour is, so is Satan.

His High Chief role, his inheritance; opposition came from within family, and even when that had been resolved, evil spread to village. But God carried him through all these trials, to be finally recognized and accepted within extended family and village.

Enemy didn't stop there, took matter to Court; had to be recognized legally, although culturally and genealogically, it was his inheritance.

God is the God of Miracles

After much delaying tactics, the Lord took over, and out of the blue, within the matter of half an hour, the Court rubber stamped and officially recognized him in eyes of law as the High Chief for his family and village. 8:30 a.m. yesterday.

Last Friday was our Sponsors' thank-you dinner. Everything that could go wrong, did, and worst part was, we couldn't do a thing about it, as it was out of our control. The dinner was put on by the Dept., and we just had to accept, and trust in the Lord. God is the God of miracles, and what may seem disaster for us, He turns into overwhelming success, that it just blows our minds away.

Monday met up with some of Sponsors, and they were very happy, said what a wonderful time they had, it was their fellowship, meeting and talking with one another. They didn't notice the cramped condition and physical flaws we knew.

Praise God for loving us so much!

God is Watching Over Us

Sunday, service of fasting & prayer. Although enemies always trying to catch us out; but our God is watching over us, and turns what Satan has in store for us, into good for His children. Yesterday my daughter rang excited, received an A+ for her last drama presentation. She is preparing for her final submissions, and exams.

Thank you so much for your faithful prayers, truly we could not have got this far without your intercession, and faithful prayers. We pray our Lord Jesus Christ continue to intensify his anointing upon you all, for His service and glory!

-Tifi (Samoa)

---

*"What is there in the earth worth living for
but the glory of God and the salvation of souls?"*

"Expect great things from God; attempt great things for God."

*"I'm not afraid of failure;
I'm afraid of succeeding at things that don't matter."*

*"Prayer -- secret, fervent, believing prayer -- lies at the root of all
personal godliness."*

-William Carey (1761-1834)
Welsh Missionary to India

172

Oct. 23, 2006 - Answer to Prayer:

I've been ill for the past three weeks, lots of severe pain in my heart.   Placed into Hospital Emergency last Thursday, Oct. 19. Transferred to Hospital in New Westminster on Friday, Oct. 20; had minor heart surgery, where they put a stint into my main vein that leads into my heart, that was 70% blocked.

I claimed healing from God, especially from Psalm 9, and especially Verse 2. I Praise God in the name of Jesus for healing me, as I was sent home on Saturday completely *okay!*

-Lay Monk Ed (British Columbia, Canada)

Nov. 14, 2006 - Prayer Request:

Please pray for our own Lay Monk Bob, 80 years old, who is quite weak; recovering from a heart attack and severe gout in both feet, to where he cannot walk. He greatly needs your prayers.

-The Lay Monks (Vancouver, Washington)

Answer to Prayer - Jan. 4, 2007

I have been healed, and am now back out on the streets of Portland, Oregon, preaching Salvation through Jesus. Thank you for your prayers, and thanks to Jesus for healing me.

-Lay Monk Bob (Portland, Oregon)

Note: Lay Monk Bob, one of the four original members of our ministry, would live to preach the Good News of Jesus daily on the streets of Portland, Oregon, and in missionary journeys to Mexico, for another nine years before he went home to be with his Lord.

"If you ask, 'Why is this happening? no light may come,
but if you ask, 'How am I to glorify God now?
there will always be an answer."

-J.I. Packer (1926-2020)
Author: *Knowing God*

Feb. 2, 2007 - Answer to Prayer:

Alleluia! Praise the Lord! Praise and glory be to God! For He has answered my prayers!

I still have my job, in spite of the sexual harassment case that was wrongly lodged against me.

My discipline was a two-day suspension without pay. All of this, for just being too nice, too friendly, and too child-like, to a female co-worker. Glory be to the Father, and to the Son, and to the Holy Spirit!

-Hector

Mar. 20, 2007 - Prayer Request:

My grandson is in the hospital with pneumonia and other complications. He is six years old, and doesn't seem to be responding to medication. Please pray for a full recovery, in the name of Jesus Christ.

God bless you, -Ed (New Jersey)

Mar. 21, 2007 – Answer to Prayer (One day later.)

Prayer was answered, grandson is coming home today! They at the hospital could not understand how he got better so quickly: I do. Thank you, Jesus.

God bless all that prayed. -Ed (New Jersey)

April 15, 2007 - Prayer Request:

Please pray for our own Lay Monk Bob, 80 years old, who has a two-inch black scab on his right hand that looks very Cancerous, and for any other problems that we cannot see (he is one of those people who will not go to a Doctor).

We will be fasting about this matter this week, and invite any others worldwide who would like to join us in this, for one or more days.

-The Lay Monks (Vancouver, Washington)

S.G. Preston

Answer to Prayer - April 21, 2007 (Six Days Later.)

All praise to God! All the black is gone, there is only a little scarring covering about one-fifth of the original area.

Thank you so much for your prayers, and especially those who joined us in fasting.

-The Lay Monks (Vancouver, Washington)

The Lord's Prayer

*"Our Divine Instructor would not teach us
to pray for impossibilities;
He puts such petitions into our mouths
as can be heard and answered.*

*Yet certainly this is a great prayer;
it has the hue of the infinite about it."*

-Charles Spurgeon (1834-1892)
English Baptist; "The Prince of Preachers"

———

*"Jesus told His Disciples not only how to pray, but what to pray.
If they pray this prayer, God will certainly hear them.*

*The Lord's Prayer is the quintessence of Prayer.
A Disciple's prayer is founded on and circumscribed by it.*

*Once again Jesus does not leave His Disciples in ignorance;
He teaches them The Lord's Prayer and so leads them to a clear
understanding of prayer."*

*"It would not be difficult to arrange all of the Psalms
according to the petitions of the Lord's Prayer.
We should need to change only slightly
our arrangement of the order of the sections."*

-Dietrich Bonhoeffer (1906-1945) German Lutheran
Author: *Psalms: The Prayer Book of the Bible*
and *The Cost of Discipleship*

175

7.2 Head of State Better, Received IT Job, Hired in Uganda

*"I prayed in the woods
and on the mountain,
even before dawn.*

*I felt no hurt from the snow
or ice or rain."*

-St. Patrick (c. 385-461 A.D.)

———

*"For as the rain comes down from heaven,
and the snow from heaven...
so shall My word be that
goes out of my mouth:*

*it shall not return to me empty,
but it shall accomplish
that which I please,
and it shall prosper in the thing
to which I sent it."*

-Isaiah 55:10-11

April 27, 2007 - Answer to Prayer

Hallelujah, praise be to God, for He truly answers prayers. My daughter, whom I requested prayers for her exam, received A+ grade. Thank you for your faithful prayers for our Chaplain. Everything went off well, and God's message was swift and powerful.

Thank you for your faithful prayers; my daughter, whom I requested prayers for, has been successful with her application. She is now the new CEO for our Tourism. May God continue to intensify his anointing upon you all, as prayer warriors for our Lord Jesus Christ!

-Tifi (Samoa)

———————————

S.G. Preston

April 29, 2007 - Prayer Request:

Please pray for K., who was injured Saturday, 28th April, and has not recovered consciousness. Please cover his wife and two children. We call upon our Lord, the Healer of all Healers; *by His stripes* we claim K.'s healing.

-Tifi (Samoa)

Answer to Prayer (Three Days Later.) Received May 3, 2007

Praise God, our merciful and loving Healer. Had requested prayers for K.; was in coma since Saturday, 28th April. Tuesday, 1st May, between 12 a.m. and 2 a.m., he began to recover consciousness.

Wednesday, 2nd May, he was taken from intensive care, to *Out of Danger* ward. I thank God for your faithful prayers. God bless you all! Praise God our Healer, the God who answers prayers.

-Tifi (Samoa)

May 6, 2007 - Prayer Request:

Please pray for our Head of State. Because of his age, he is not able to discharge fluid easily; thus build-up of fluid. Please pray for equipment to be installed at his home, also medical care provided on home basis; so he is not having to move around, and be transported to and from hospital.

He is 95, and finding it more difficult to cope with hospital surroundings. May *Jehovah Rapha,* our Healer, just touch him, and renew his strength like an eagle. The Lord has blessed him with long life for a purpose. It was his forefather who first received the Good News and Salvation of Jesus Christ, from missionary John Williams; and so conversion of our whole country.

If it his time to go home, God's will be done, otherwise, the Lord knows our hearts. We stand on his Word: *by His stripes we are healed*, and may His healing of our Head of State be an even greater witness to our country, and all people, that God is alive, and draw more souls to his kingdom. Thank you, God bless!

-Tifi (Samoa)

Answer to Prayer - May 7, 2007 (Later That Same Day.)

Around about 11 p.m. last night Samoan time, our Head of State's condition changed miraculously for the better.

His condition took a turn for the worse yesterday evening, but God is faithful; about 12 a.m. last night a miracle occurred, and his condition began to improve.

I know God has healed him, and his healing is progressing right now.

Thank you, -Tifi (Samoa)

May 11, 2007 - Answer to Prayer:

Tu. has regained consciousness, and had first taste of food this evening. Thank you for your faithful prayers, God bless and intensify His anointing upon you for His service.

-Tifi (Samoa)

June 1, 2007 - Answer to Prayer:

Dear Brothers and Sisters, God has blessed me. I have gotten a new job with great pay and benefits.

I will be on 90 day probation; then my insurance will kick in.

It is temporary to permanent, 40 hours a week.

This job sounds a lot easier; even though I never have sold IT solutions, I believe God will guide me and help me through the training, so that I can learn it and apply it to all my sales, and be able to make the funds I need to support my family.

I have gotten involved in our community; in *Citizens on Patrol*; seeking funds to assist our residents with emergencies.

We even have a church service in our Community Center with Bible classes for everyone.

Thanks; have a wonderful Jesus day, -Libbie

S.G. Preston

Nov. 11, 2006 - Prayer Request:

Have just completed a PhD, but have been struggling to find employment in my country, due to being over-qualified...however, I have absolute faith that God is turning this around. I pray, and ask you to pray with me, that God will *open doors for me, that no man can close*; that He *will make a way, where there seems to be no way.*

That He *will surround me with His favor as a shield, for with God nothing is impossible*; and that He will provide a good, satisfying job for me, in Jesus' Mighty Name. -Suzanne (Uganda)

Answer to Prayer - February, 2007 (Ten Weeks Later.)
Received June 15, 2007

Dear Brothers at the *PrayerFoundation*,™ I hope you are well. I did not want to be like the lepers who did not come back to say thanks. I to give a praise report!!! I submitted a prayer request in November, for a job...at that time, I had been offered a one month job, at the same place I am in right now.

Well when my one month was over, I was requested to work for another month, with the assurance that they could simply not afford to keep me on. As the second month elapsed, a call for proposals from the WHO came in, and I was encouraged by my boss to submit a proposal...this proposal was granted in February, 2007, offering me a three year job on a small, challenging but rewarding area in Health Sciences.

Yes, the work I am doing is challenging, but I know that God's ways are higher than mine, and His thoughts far above mine. It is the *perfect* job...you see, while I was applying for jobs before...and got all these interviews which stressed me, yet all those times I did not really feel I even wanted the jobs I was being interviewed for...I just wanted any job.

God in all His mercy and goodness, saw fit to hold me back, until a job came along which would offer emotional, intellectual (career), and material satisfaction...*He Is A Good God!!!*

What amazes me even more is that this job was offered to me without my even filling out an application, or doing an interview.

I am praying for wisdom, favor, and excellence at this job...and that all the work I do may bring glory to God. Well, that is my praise report, and I thank you for praying for me, and with me. May God bless you richly and keep you always.

Yours in Christ, -Suzanne (Uganda)

To the Director of Music: a Psalm of David.

**O LORD, You have examined my heart, and have known me.
You know me when I sit down, and when I rise up.**
You understand my thoughts from far away.

You surround me on my path, and when I lay down;
You are acquainted with all my ways.
Before I even speak a word; You, O LORD,
already know what I will say.

You surround me with Your presence;
Your hand rests upon me.
This knowledge is too wonderful for me;
it is so high above me,
that I cannot fully comprehend it.

**Where shall I go to escape from Your Spirit?
Where shall I flee to hide from Your presence?**
If I ascend up to heaven, You are there.
If I make my bed in Hell, behold, You are there.

If I fly away on the wings of the morning,
to make my home in the farthest parts of the sea;
even there Your hands shall guide me,
and Your right hand shall be my support.

If I say, "Surely the darkness shall cover me,"
then even the darkness shall be like light around me.
Yes, the darkness cannot hide me from You.
The night shines for You like the day;
the darkness and the light are both alike to You.

-Psalm 139:1-12

180

7.3 Indonesia Blessings, House Sells, Russian Seminary Certified

"Thus will thought pray without ceasing;
if thought prays not only in words,
but unite yourself to God
through all the course of life
and so your life be made
one ceaseless and
uninterrupted
prayer."

-St. Basil the Great (329-379 A.D.)

———

"Let us therefore go boldly to the Throne of Grace,
so that we may obtain mercy,
and find grace to help in time of need."

-Hebrews 4:16

July 5, 2007 - Answer to Prayer:

...and now, I'm walking with a cane; *not* the walker! My first steps in 9 months! *Praise God, from whom all blessings flow!*

-(Lay Monk) Pastor Roger

———————————————

July 7, 2007 - Answer to Prayer:

Praise report! Thanks to Jesus for His love in this retreat. Thanks to all my friends, and all people all over the world that have prayed for us, the Catholic Renewal community in Indonesia.

I have seen and heard many testimonials about experiencing the love of God, and of the Holy Spirit; many young men and women have felt the love of God in this retreat.

Jesus love you all, -Okky (Indonesia)

———————————————

July 24, 2007 – Answer to Prayer:

Praise Report: Thank you Brothers, for your prayers. I asked that you would pray that I sell my house, so I could move back home.

I am not sure what the exact date was, when I asked for prayer; but in less than 2 weeks I had an offer on my house.

Thank you all for your prayers, you are a true blessing from our Lord. -Jim (Alabama)

Aug. 18, 2007 - Prayer Request

Our Seminary in Russia, *****, will have a visit from the Sanitation Department.

The visit will be led by *****, who just last week began a conversation with our Provost *****, with the following words:

> "I remember you.
> I still don't like you (from the last visit)…
> Why are you poisoning our young people?
> You are not Russian Orthodox!"

Although ***** did his best to disarm the situation, it still set the tone for the remainder of the conversation.

***** negotiated further with her. She agreed to visit the Seminary for an inspection.

As it turns out, she has enough clout in her department to say either, "I close your building down" or: "I will certify your building."

So we at *****, request for your prayers. Please pray for this Inspector.

May God turn her heart toward us, so that she will not do something against us, but rather do all the paper work the way we need for the licensing process.

Thank you very much in advance, for your prayers.

*****, President
***** Seminary

S.G. Preston

Answer to Prayer - Aug. 22, 2007 (Four Days Later.)

We have some great news from Moscow! Today, ***** from the Sanitary Department, came to inspect the Seminary. As ***** came to the school, ***** welcomed her at the door, and noticed a change in her demeanor. Today she was friendly and very accommodating.

Obviously, she had a change of attitude about the Seminary, and approached today's business with an open mind. She toured various sections of the Seminary, and pointed out only one minor issue that needed to be corrected: too many computers in the lab.

The classrooms, offices, and the library were all approved without a problem -- thus all of the rooms used for *educational purposes* are now certified. We are now breathing a big sigh of relief. Thank you for your prayers on our behalf! And perhaps the biggest answer to prayer?

Because ***** was late for her next appointment, she asked ***** to drive back to her office (she had taken public transportation to the school). ***** gladly complied, and an interesting and engaging conversation took place in the car, that eventually focused on the faith.

A friend of hers had converted to the *Adventist* movement and ***** had several questions. ***** took advantage of the moment, and shared with her about his faith.

As ***** told me: "We talked about Christ Jesus, about the way of Salvation, about His Death and Resurrection, and about common things between Russian Orthodoxy and Evangelicals (i.e., His Resurrected Life and 2nd Coming). Wonderful, just wonderful! Glory to God! Hallelujah! Praise Him!"

Last week, she was antagonistic against Evangelicals. Today, she was openly engaged in a conversation about the faith. Such a change in her disposition can only have come through the Holy Spirit! Thank you for your prayers. Sincerely,

*****, President
***** Seminary

183

Aug. 19, 2007 - Prayer Request:

Good day and may God bless you. I thank God for you in advance.

I have written your ministry twice now, requesting prayer for my marriage to my wife, and for her. As I said, she had requested a TRO be placed against me, based on sins that are long past, and she knows that. I am a pacifist, and a Bible believing man of God, and am sober now.

The court date is on Monday at 8:00 a.m., Hawaii Standard Time (3 hours after California, I think). Please intercede for us then, and if she doesn't show up, then no TRO.

I just want God's Will and His Word performed in this matter, and am believing Him for the victory already in my marriage, and restoration of my household back to me. Thank you and your ministry for your help.

Your brother in Christ, -Richard (Hawaii)

Answer to Prayer - Aug. 22, 2007 (Three days Later.)

Good day, and may God bless all you people who have held my marriage and my wife up to God in prayer. I wanted to inform you all of what happened at the TRO court hearing at 8:00 this morning.

My wife requested a one year restraining order against me based primarily on past sins from years ago.

We are both Bible believing, and I asked for promotion and purification so...I requested four months, and mom to be with our two sons for visitation, and marital counseling.

Her request was granted by the Judge, in whom I see no fault. And she didn't look into my eyes, but hers have looked better. I prayed that God's will be done, and it is.

The good news is, she can request the court dissolve or amend the TRO at any time during this year. She is also going to be going to our church, at a service I won't go to. And I am surrendering it all to Jesus. I may go to Israel to serve, if He lets me, but otherwise I plan on being hopeful, faithful to her, and sober minded.

184

S.G. Preston

I wanted to say thank you, and thank God for each and every one of you, who took time out of your schedules to answer when I called. I am assured that God's Will be done in this. Bless you all again, in Jesus' Name, Amen.

Your brother in Christ, -Richard (Hawaii)

For You have created me inside and out,
You have woven me together in my mother's womb.
I will praise You, for I am fearfully and wonderfully made.
All Your works are wonderful; I am fully aware of this.

The forming of my body was not hidden from You,
when I was created in secret, and my body intricately
woven together in my mother's womb.
Your eyes beheld my embryo, when it was still unformed.

The number of my days was already written
and recorded in the scroll of Your book,
when none of them had yet been brought into existence.

How precious are Your thoughts toward me, O God!
How great is the sum of them!
If I should try to count them, they are more in number than the
grains of sand; and when I awake, I am still with You.

Examine me, O God, and know my heart;
test me, and know my thoughts.
Reveal to me if there is any wicked way in me,
and lead me in the path to everlasting life.

-Psalm 139:13-18, 23-24

"In ordinary life we hardly realize that we receive a great deal more
than we give, and that it is only with gratitude
that life becomes rich."

-Dietrich Bonhoeffer (1906-1945) Theologian, Nazi Resistor
Author: *Psalms: The Prayer Book of the Bible*
and *The Cost of Discipleship*

7.4 Promoted in India, Grandma Better, Healing in U.K.

*"We should not seek so much to pray,
but to become prayer."*

-St. Francis of Assisi (1181/1182-1226 A.D.)

———

*"In my distress I called upon the LORD,
and cried out to my God:
He heard my voice from His Temple,
and my cry arrived before Him,
even into His ears."*

-Psalm 18:6

Oct. 6, 2007 - Prayer Request:

Please pray that I be promoted to Level 5, so that I can be able to keep supporting my family.

-Anand. (Chennai, India)

Answer to Prayer - Jan. 8, 2008

After four months, I have finally been promoted to Level 5! Thank you so much -- this means all the difference in the world for the support of my family!

-Anand. (Chennai, India)

———

Dec. 25, 2007 - Prayer Request:

Dear Brothers, I would like to ask prayer for my friend's mom. Grandma is 84 years old and has just had a spleen-dectomy, her blood platelets were down due to lupus, and a pacemaker fitted.

She is now coming down with an infection. She is already weak from the surgery and needs to heal. Can you please pray for her healing? Can you also pray peace into this family? God is slowly drawing them all towards a real faith in him.

186

My friend is returning to her first love, and her son is considering going to Bible School and witnessing to friends, and other parts of the family are returning to church.

I am hoping that God would draw this entire family to Him, and that somehow Grandma's illness would be used by God to do this. I know ultimately, we need His Will. I want to thank you. I will email, and let you know how this works out.

Love and Thanks and Prayers, -Mo (Canada)

Answer to Prayer (The Same Day: Christmas Day.) Received December 28, 2007

Dear Friends, I placed a prayer request, a couple of days ago, and wanted to update you on it. It was for my friend's Grandma. She really picked up on Christmas Day, and the family had a wonderful time together.

On another note, the whole family found themselves together at church on Christmas Eve, which is such wonderful answered prayer.

Thank you. -Mo (Canada)

Mar. 18, 2008 - Answer to Prayer:

I asked for you to pray with me for Sarah, a mighty woman of the Lord, for healing from Skin Cancer. I have heard she is looking very well, and years younger. Thank you so much for praying with me for her. You are in my prayers. God Bless. In Christ,

-Victoria (London, U.K.)

May 28, 2008 - Answer to Prayer:

Blessings! Your ministry started praying for me, when I began a special daily shot of Interferon to fight cirrhosis scarring, and bring my Hepatitis C viral level down. I began this about 8-9 weeks ago, as you may recall, and have had some good results. Initially: I lost nearly 20 pounds, and developed anemia along with other side-effects.

Praise God; my last blood work showed a 200-fold drop in Hep. C viral load in only 1 month; Normal Tests is for a client doing well to have a 100-fold drop after 3 full months. My Dr. took labs. after a month, showing a drop from 2 million to 1,100; a level that takes others three or more months to reach, and many don't reach at all.

My weight is also gradually going up, and per my Dr., there are no traces of anemia. Also, the Lord is blessing me financially. When I turned 55 in April, I had three retirement funds made available to me. I rolled them over into a trading account, starting with about 30K.

I hope that this will help supplement my disability insurance (although I won't touch any profits until 59 1/2 due to taxes), and ask that you pray that I have wisdom. My purpose is not to become rich but to have more to give away; even on disability I never give less than 10%, and sometimes up to 20+% a month. I am on track for a healthier summer, and pray that you are too.

-Brother Rick (Brooklyn, New York)
Ps. 118:17

Sept 5, 2008 - Answer to Prayer:

I asked for Lay Monk Linda to pray for me, as I am / was recovering from rape which turned my life upside down over the last few years.

Within a few weeks I came across a Catholic priest who I spoke to in the U.S.A., who helped me immensely. I then came across a woman in the U.S.A. who I spoke to, who helped even more with the emotions.

It is incredible. I am feeling peace of mind, joy and have hope for the future. I never believed this could really happen. I feel so much healing has been received, and health in mind and soul / spirit. My head is clear and calm, for the first time in years.

Thank you so much for your prayer! Your ministry is in my prayers.

In Christ, God Bless. ***** (U.K.)

S.G. Preston

Nov. 6, 2008 - Answer to Prayer:

I praise and give thanks to God, that he gave me a nice job in a top company (i.e., in software testing tools: Q.T.P.), and made me able to move to the U.S.A. in 2008.

-Daniel (California)

To the Director of Music: a Psalm of David.

Deliver me, O LORD, from the evil person;
protect me from the violent person.
They devise troublemaking in their hearts;
they are continually gathered together for war.
Their throat is an open tomb; they deceive with their tongue;
the poison of vipers is under their lips. Selah.

Protect me, O LORD, from the hands of the wicked.
Preserve me from the violent person; for they plot against me
to make me stumble and fall, to destroy me.
The arrogant have hidden a snare for me, with their ropes.
They have spread out their net by the side of the road,
and have set traps for me. Selah.

I said to the LORD, "You are my God.
Hear the sound of my supplications, O LORD.
O God, the LORD, the strength of my salvation,
You have protected my head in the day of battle.
Do not grant the desires of the wicked O LORD.
Do not further their wicked plots.
Do not let them exalt themselves." Selah.

-Psalm 140:1-8

———

"We pray for the big things and forget to give thanks
for the small (and yet really not small) gifts."

-Dietrich Bonhoeffer (1906-1945) Lutheran Pastor, Martyr
Author: *Psalms: The Prayer Book of the Bible*
and *The Cost of Discipleship*

189

7.5 Dear *PrayerFoundation* ™

Fantastic Site, very interesting on how early Irish Monks would marry and have a family. Explains a lot about the origins of the surnames O Reachtabhra (Rafferty) and O Reachtabhair (Rafter), as a majority of men with the personal name Reachtabhra in the 7th-9th centuries were Abbots.

Beir Bua Agus Beannacht (Bring Victory and Blessing).

-Gary (County Cork, Republic of Ireland)

My name is Paul. I have contacted you before, a couple years ago. I have visited your website many times since then. The desire to lead a life of prayer, simplicity and evangelism has only grown stronger.

I am currently serving in the U.S. Navy, but will soon be a seminary student at *Covenant Theological Seminary* in St. Louis, Missouri.

I want to say that your website is fantastic! It is loaded with great information. I like the way you use the Psalms for prayer. I would stay up all night checking out your website, but I have to get to sleep.

I am deployed to ***** currently, and I have watch very early in the morning. I hope to hear back from you.

God bless you, -Paul

Marvelous Site! I am content to be acquainted with people that honour the Word of God, and at same time appreciate the movies, especially those with Christian subjects.

Here in Brazil, Believers avoid movie theaters, television, and magazines with photos of actors and actresses.

Movie pictures for them are worldly. I think it is exaggeration, because there are good films and bad films, as there are good and bad books.

190

S.G. Preston

Certainly, you must be pleased about your marvelous website *PrayerFoundation,*™ with a section dedicated for excellent analysis of the movies.

I know all the Hollywood masterpieces of the fifties that had an important part to confirm my Christian faith, in my young years.

I see them with great satisfaction in your list of the Top Ten Best Christian Films ever made by Hollywood in the golden age.

...great information and wise advice you give for all your happy visitors. God bless you and your splendid work!

Sincerely, -Claudio (Brazil)

Gave up the website *Requests4Prayers* due to health and being inundated by evil emails and Site attacks. Donation on way.

-Lay Monk Vince (Colorado)

Dear Lay Monks, I start each day with Bible, Prayer, and Brother Juniper. Great idea, that one!

Yours truly, -Lay Monk William

Note: Brother Juniper is the Cartoon posted on our website (prayerfoundation.net).

As for those who surround me,
let the troublemaking of their own lips cover them.

Do not let an evil speaker be established in the earth;
evil shall hunt the violent person to overthrow them.

**I know that the LORD will maintain
the cause of the afflicted,
and the right of the poor.**

The godly shall give thanks to Your name.
The upright shall dwell in Your presence.

-Psalm 140:9, 11-13

191

7.6 C.S. Lewis: *Modern Theology and Biblical Criticism*

"All theology of the liberal type
involves at some point -
and often involves throughout -

the claim that the real behavior
and purpose and teaching of Christ
came very rapidly to be misunderstood
and misrepresented by his followers,
and has been recovered or exhumed
only by modern scholars."

-C.S. Lewis (1898-1963)
Author: *Mere Christianity*

"And yet they would often sound - if you didn't know the truth - extremely convincing.

Many reviewers suggested that the Ring in Tolkien's *The Lord of the Rings* was suggested by the atom bomb. What could be more plausible? Yet in fact, the chronology of the book's composition makes the theory impossible.

Only the other week a reviewer said that a fairy-tale by my friend Roger Lancelyn Green was influenced by fairy-tales of mine. Nothing could be more probable. I have an imaginary country with a beneficent lion in it; Green, one with a beneficent tiger. Green and I can be proved to read one another's works...

The case for an affiliation is far stronger than many which we accept as conclusive when dead authors are concerned.

But it's all untrue nevertheless. I know the genesis of that Tiger and that Lion and they are quite independent.

The reconstruction of the history of a text, when the text is ancient, sounds very convincing. But one is after all sailing by dead reckoning; the results cannot be checked by fact.

192

In order to decide how reliable the method is, what more could you ask for than to be shown an instance where the same method is at work and we have facts to check it by?

Well, that is what I have done.

And we find, that when this check is available, the results are either always, or else nearly always, wrong.

The 'assured results of modern scholarship' as to the way in which an old book was written, are 'assured', we may conclude, only because the men who know the facts are dead and can't blow the gaff.

...We think that different elements in this sort of theology have different degrees of strength.

The nearer it sticks to mere textual criticism, of the old sort, Lachmann's sort, the more we are disposed to believe in it.

And of course, we agree that passages almost verbally identical cannot be independent.

It is as we glide away from this into reconstructions of a subtler and more ambitious kind that our faith in the method waivers; and our faith in Christianity is proportionally corroborated.

The sort of statement that arouses our deepest skepticism is the statement that something in a Gospel cannot be historical because it shows a theology or an ecclesiology too developed for so early a date.

For this implies that we know, first of all, that there was any development in the matter, and secondly, how quickly it proceeded.

It even implies an extraordinary homogeneity and continuity of development: implicitly denies that anyone could have greatly anticipated anyone else.

This seems to involve knowing about a number of long dead people -- for the early Christians were, after all, people -- things of which I believe few of us could have given an accurate account if we had lived among them; all the forward and backward surge of discussion, preaching, and individual religious experience.

Such are the reactions of one bleating layman to Modern Theology.

Once the layman was anxious to hide the fact that he believed so much less than the vicar; now he tends to hide the fact that he believes so much more.

Missionary to the priests of one's own church is an embarrassing role; though I have a horrid feeling that if such mission work is not soon undertaken the future history of the Church of England is likely to be short."

-Excerpted from: *Modern Theology and Biblical Criticism*
by C.S. Lewis. Lewis read this Essay at
Westcott House, Cambridge, on 11 May 1959.
Published under this title in *Christian Reflections*; 1981.
It is now included in *Fern-Seed and Elephants*; 1998.

"I am trying here to prevent anyone saying the really foolish thing that people often say about Him:

'I'm ready to accept Jesus as a great moral teacher, but I don't accept His claim to be God.'

That is the one thing we must not say.

A man who was merely a man and said the sort of things Jesus said would not be a great moral teacher.

He would either be a lunatic -- on the level with a man who says he is a poached egg -- or else he would be the Devil of Hell.

You must make your choice.

Either this man was, and is, the Son of God, or else a madman or something worse.

You can shut Him up for a fool, you can spit at Him and kill Him as a demon or you can fall at His feet and call Him Lord and God,

but let us not come with any patronizing nonsense about His being a great human teacher.

He has not left that open to us. He did not intend to."

-C.S. Lewis; *Mere Christianity* (Book II, Chapter 3)

7.7 C.S. Lewis (1898-1963): Thoughts

*"The only safety is to have a standard
of plain, central Christianity
("mere Christianity" as Baxter called it)
which puts the controversies of the moment
in their proper perspective."*

———

*"The Son of God became a man
to enable men to become sons of God."*

———

"Joy is the serious business of heaven."

———

***"Do not imagine that if you meet a really humble man
he will be what most people call 'humble' nowadays:***
*he will not be a sort of greasy, smarmy person,
who is always telling you that, of course, he is nobody.*

*Probably all you will think about him is that he seemed a cheerful,
intelligent chap who took a real interest in what you said to him.*

*If you do dislike him it will be because you feel
a little envious of anyone who seems to enjoy life so easily.*

*He will not be thinking about humility:
he will not be thinking about himself at all.*

***If anyone would like to acquire humility,
I can, I think, tell him the first step.***

The first step is to realise that one is proud.

*And a biggish step, too.
At least, nothing whatever can be done before it.*

*If you think you are not conceited,
it means you are very conceited indeed."*

* * *

7.8 Christ's Judgment for Believers is Only for Reward

Because Jesus' Shed Blood Paid the Price for Every Single One of Our Sins

*"But to you that reverence My name,
the Sun of Righteousness shall arise
with healing in His wings;*

*and you shall go free,
leaping about like calves
let out to pasture."*

-Malachi 4:2

The Blood of Jesus Christ His Son Cleanses Us From All Sin (1 John 1:7)

*"Having therefore boldness to enter into the Holy of Holies,
by the blood of Jesus;"* -Hebrews 4:16

———

*"Let us then go boldly to the throne of grace, so that we can receive
mercy, and find grace to help in time of need."* -Hebrews 10:1

———

*"Therefore being justified by faith, we have peace with God
through our Lord Jesus Christ:"* -Romans 5:1

———

"I will remember their sins no more." -Hebrews 8:12

———

*"I tell you the truth: whoever hears My word
and believes Him who sent Me,
has eternal life and will not be condemned;
they have crossed over from death to life."* -John 5:24

———

"...for the one that comes to God must believe that He is,
and that He is a rewarder of those
that diligently seek Him." -Hebrews 11:6

———

"For we are His workmanship,
created in Christ Jesus to do good works,
which God has before ordained
that we should walk in them." -Ephesians 2:10

———

"And behold, I will arrive quickly; and My reward is with Me,
to give to everyone according to their work." -Revelation 22:12

———

"For other foundation can no one lay
than that which is laid, which is Jesus Christ.

Now if anyone build upon this foundation gold, silver,
precious stones, wood, hay, stubble;
everyone's work shall be made manifest:
for the Day shall declare it,
because it shall be revealed by fire;
and the fire shall test everyone's work; of what sort it is.

If anyone's work, which they have built,
remains, they shall receive a reward.

If anyone's work shall be burned, they shall suffer loss;
but they themselves shall be saved;" -1 Corinthians 3:11-15

———

"His Lord said to him,
'Well done, good and faithful servant;
you have been faithful over a few things;
I will make you ruler over many things;
enter into the joy of your Lord.'"

-Matthew 25:23

* * *

7.9 Lay Monk Thoughts: Son of God in O.T. & N.T.

Son of God in the Old Testament

*"Search the Scriptures,
for in them you think you have eternal life,
and they are the same Scriptures
that testify of Me."*

-John 5:39

———

*"Then He said to them, 'How foolish you are,
and slow to believe all that the prophets have spoken.*

*Did not the Messiah have to suffer these things,
and then enter into His glory?'*

*And beginning with Moses and all the prophets,
He explained to them what was said
in all the Scriptures concerning Himself."*

-Luke 24:25-27

God's Son

Does the Old Testament specifically state that God has a Son? Yes, it does (Boldface mine.):

*"Who has ascended up into heaven, or descended?
Who has gathered the wind in his fists?
Who has wrapped up the waters in His cloak?*

*What is His name,
and **what is His Son's name?**
Surely you know!"*

-Proverbs 30:4

*"Out of Egypt, I have called **My Son**."*

-Hosea 11:1; Matthew 2:15

198

*"For unto us a child is born, unto us a **Son** is given,*
and the government shall be upon His shoulder;
and His name shall be called, Wonderful, Counselor,
the mighty God, the everlasting Father, the Prince of Peace."

-Isaiah 9:6

Psalm 2

This Psalm is a prophecy about the Incarnation of Christ, and His Second Advent (Return). It foretells the alliance of Herod, Pilate, and the Sanhedrin against God's Messiah; God's King, God's Son:

Why do the nations rage, and the people imagine a foolish thing?
The kings of the earth set themselves;
yes, the rulers take counsel together,
against the LORD, and against His Messiah, saying:
"Let us break their chains apart, and cast their ropes away from us."

He that sits in the heavens shall laugh: the LORD shall mock them.
Then He shall speak to them in His wrath,
and trouble them in His great displeasure, announcing:
"I have set My King upon my holy hill of Zion."

This King will proclaim:
"I will declare the decree: **'The LORD has said to Me:**
'You are My Son, this day I have begotten You.' "

"Ask of Me, and I shall give You the nations for your inheritance,
and the farthest parts of the earth for Your possession.
You shall break them with a rod of iron;
You shall break them in pieces like pottery."

Therefore be wise now, O you kings;
be instructed, you who are judges on the earth.
Serve the LORD with reverence, and rejoice in trembling awe.

Honor the Son, lest He become angry,
and you perish from the way,
when His wrath is kindled suddenly.
Blessed are all those that
put their trust in Him."

199

Son of God in the New Testament

"God has fulfilled the same to us, their children,
in that He has raised up Jesus again;
as it is also written in the second Psalm:

*'**You are my Son,** this day I have begotten You.'"*

-Acts 13:33

The Son of God

"And the angel answered, saying to her:
'The Holy Spirit shall rest upon you,
and the power of the Highest shall overshadow you;
therefore the holy child who shall be born of you
*shall be called **the Son of God**.'"*

-Luke 1:35

———

"Simon Peter answered, saying,
*'You are the Messiah, **the Son of the Living God**.'*

And Jesus said to him,
'Blessed are you, Simon Bar Jonah; for flesh and blood have not
revealed this to you; but my Father, who is in Heaven.'"

-Matthew 16:16-17

———

"Paul. a servant of Jesus Christ, called to be an apostle,
separated to the Gospel of God, which He had promised before
by His prophets in the Holy Scriptures.

*Concerning **His Son Jesus Christ our Lord**, who was made of the*
seed of David according to the flesh; and declared to be
***the Son of God** with power, according to the Spirit of Holiness,*
by His resurrection from the dead..."

-Romans 1:1-4

* * *

200

8. *The LORD Our Righteousness (Yahweh Tsidkenu)*

8.1 Promoted in Philippines, Out of Coma in U.K., Hired in U.A.E.

*"It is simply impossible to lead,
without the aid of prayer,
a virtuous life."*

-St. John Chrysostom (c. 347-407 A.D.)
Monk, Patriarch of Constantinople

———

*"You have not chosen Me,
but I have chosen you, and ordained you,
that you should go and bring forth fruit,
and that your fruit should remain:
that whatever you shall ask of the Father
in My name, He may give it to you."*

-John 15:16

Nov. 7, 2008 - Answer to Prayer

Thanks a ton for your prayers, I have got my promotion letter...

-Flora (Philippines)

———

Jan. 4, 2009 - Prayer Request:

Please pray for me. I have been unemployed since August, and my Unemployment Extension has been delayed. I don't know how I'm going to live? If I have to live on the street, I don't know if I'll survive, I have Asthma. I am a Christian and know the Lord. Please pray that I find a job, and that my Unemployment Benefits will go through! Also, could you pray for my cat; he is sickly, and I have to buy his medicine; he's my little buddy, and I don't want to see him die!!

Yours in Christ...thank you... -Darrell (Kingman, Arizona)

Answer to Prayer - Jan. 6, 2009 (Two Days Later.)

Dearest Lay Monks, praise God, and thank you for your prayers. This morning I found out that my Unemployment Extension was approved. I'm back on the rolls, and now will survive! I can also buy medicine for my cat's condition! How the Lord hears the prayers of His saints! How full of mercy He is! I'm so grateful, thank you.

Yours in Christ, -Darrell (Kingman, Arizona)

May 26, 2009 - Answer to Prayer:

My accommodation was sorted out, and I agreed the rent with the landlord. Thank you. My heart is warm again and I am feeling happier. It has been 7 years since *my traumatic experience*, and I truly feel life is returning; and that I am beginning to be in the world again, and not in a pit. Thank you. I would love to visit your *Foundation* one day.

Much love in Christ, ***** (U.K.)

June 8, 2009 - Answer to Prayer:

Thank you for your prayers! Lay Monk Bob's legs have been completely healed -- He had to use a cane to go do his street preaching for several months, and was in great pain.

-The Lay Monks (Vancouver, Washington)

June 8, 2009 - Answer to Prayer:

Last year, the *PrayerFoundation* ™ joined in intercession for Ian, who had an emergency operation to remove a brain tumor. Thank the Lord for His healing; as Ian has finished the Radiology and Chemo. therapies, and been clear of Cancer for some months. He has energy for his family, is fully involved at church again, and returned to full employment. May his healing strengthen his witness, and encourage others' faith in Christ. Praise Jesus for His ministry through the stewardship of the *PrayerFoundation.* ™

-Brother Bruce (U.K.) Philippians 4:4

S.G. Preston

June 10, 2009 - Prayer Request:

Please pray for a situation where I worked and am owed $800.00, which I really need badly to pay bills, and it looks like the company is not going to pay me.

They keep putting me off, and giving me the runaround.

Please pray that God turns their minds, so that they pay me what they owe me.

-(Washington State)

Answer to Prayer - June 11, 2009 (One Day Later.)

Thank you so much for praying for me. I requested prayer only yesterday, and was stunned to receive a check for the amount owed me today.

Glory to God! -(Washington State)

Nov. 9, 2009 - Answer to Prayer:

Some weeks ago the *PrayerFoundation* ™ joined in prayer for eighteen year old Emily, who ended up in a coma following a traffic accident.

Thank the Lord, because she has regained consciousness and is beginning to speak and remember things.

Her family and friends are most thankful to the Lord for the intercessions of the *PrayerFoundation.*™

Please hold her in your prayers, that her physical healing may continue, and that she may resume growing in the ways of the Lord.

-Brother Bruce (U.K.)
John 15:7

Nov. 9, 2009 - Answer to Prayer:

I got a job at Marriott Hotel. -Biju (U.A.E.)

A Psalm of David.

**LORD I cry out to You;
hasten to hear me.**
Listen to my voice,
when I cry out to You.

**Let my prayer be set before You as incense,
and the lifting up of my hands as the evening sacrifice.**

Set a watch, O LORD, before my mouth;
keep the door of my lips.

Do not let my heart become inclined to any evil thing,
to practice evil works with people who do wickedness.
Do not let me eat of their delicacies.

Let the godly correct me; it shall be a kindness.
But do not let the oil of the sinner
anoint my head.

My prayer will be intense
in the presence of their pleasures.
When their judges are overthrown
in stony places,
they shall hear my words,
for they are sweet.

Our bones are scattered at the mouth of the grave,
as when one plows and breaks up the earth.

**But my eyes look to You:
O God, the LORD.
In You is all my trust,**
do not leave my soul destitute.

Keep me from the nets which
they have hidden to catch me,
and the traps of those who are evil.

Let the wicked fall into their own nets,
while I safely pass by them.

-Psalm 141

204

8.2 Better in Singapore, Progress in India, Healing in Australia

"The Word of God is the fulcrum
upon which the lever of prayer is placed,
and by which things are mightily moved."

-E.M. Bounds (1835-1913) Methodist Pastor
Author: *Power Through Prayer*

———

"But I say to you who hear: Love your enemies,
do good to those who hate you, bless those that curse you,
and pray for those who despitefully use you."

-Luke 6:27-28

Nov. 19, 2009 - Prayer Request:

For my landlord in Singapore to agree to the tenancy agreement, and for the new flat-share to work out well. And pray for employment in London, as soon as possible. For protection for Anna in London, who had a bad experience in India.

For Isabelle, who is feeling insecure, and grieving the loss of her mother; that she is comforted, and finds good accommodation. For me to be closer to God, and to stop thinking He hates me.

To get my life in order, now the trauma is lifted, and to have more faith...in London, and to find a church, and to get better.

In Jesus' sweet name, Amen. -(Singapore)

Answer to Prayer - Dec. 7, 2009 (Nineteen Days Later.)

I don't think God hates me anymore. I thought He said He will help me. I feel a lot better. My landlord agreed to the tenancy agreement, and I have a good flat-mate for a couple of months, and I hope a lot longer. Amen. Thank you.

In Christ, -(Singapore)

Dec. 28, 2009 - Answer to Prayer:

My 8 year-old son Allan lacks concentration, and is way behind at talking in complete sentences, like other children his age. He is often made fun of due to this infirmity. I daily place my hand upon Allan's head, and say the healing verse of Jeremiah 30:11, from the Holy Bible.

Today the Lord has wonderfully shown His miracle in Allan's life. Today was Allan's Terminals Exam results. Allan secured 74%, and stood 20th, from among the 50 children of his class. Thank you, Jesus; praise you Jesus, for the wonderful miracle in Allan's life.

-Anita (India)

Feb. 8, 2010 - Prayer Request:

I would like to ask prayer for Gianni, who lives in Sydney, Australia. He lost his only son a couple of months ago through suicide, and during that time he has been diagnosed with Cancer. Now he has a metastasis (tumor) in his head. He has great difficulty talking, and he cannot walk. On the 10th of February, Gianni is going to be operated on. Unfortunately, he does not know the Lord Jesus Christ yet.

Thank you very much, -Marga (Netherlands)

Answer to Prayer: - Feb. 22, 2010

Dear *PrayerFoundation*,™ On the 8th of February, I sent a prayer request for Gianni, who lives in Sydney, Australia. He was to be operated on his head, because of a 5 cm metastasis. Three times he has had tests, and each time they found a 5 cm tumor. Miraculously, thanks to prayer, it turned out to be only 2 cm.

The operation went very well, and he only had to stay a very short time in Intensive Care. The doctors were all very surprised!! Thank you very much! I hope this will be a seed for him, to get closer in willing to know the only true and living God.

-Marga (Netherlands)

Feb. 9, 2010 - Answer to Prayer:

Thank you very much for your prayers.

My son D. miraculously found a good paying job, he has a roof over his head, is no longer living on the streets with my three little granddaughters, and he has a clean slate.

Thank you for your prayers for my nephew T. He has started a medical school billing program, and is finally working toward being able to get off the streets, and to support himself financially.

-D. (San Dumas, California)

Feb. 16, 2010 - Answer to Prayer:

Dear friends, thank you so much for your prayers. A few months ago I asked you to pray for my husband Matt. He was spiritually down, and struggling with daily life.

He was under tremendous pressure from work. In the last few weeks our situation has changed. He has finished a few projects and required examinations.

His spirits are up, and he is spiritually encouraged. For the first time in a year, he made a comment about looking forward to the future. God has worked in his spirit. Thank you for praying.

God bless you. -Susanne (Switzerland)

Feb. 18, 2010 - Answer to Prayer (Two Days Later.)

Dear *PrayerFoundation,*™

I would like to inform you that God has answered the prayers, and we won a contract with the Government agency, two days after my petitions.

Thanks to you and your *Prayer Warriors,* for interceding on my behalf.

Warm regards, -James (Miami)

A Maskil (Meditation) of David:
a Prayer when he was in the cave.

I cried out to the LORD with my voice.
With my voice, I made my supplication to the LORD.

I poured out my complaint before Him;
I showed Him my trouble.

When my spirit was overwhelmed within me,
then You showed me which way to go.

On the path in which I walk,
they have secretly set a trap for me.
I looked on my right hand,
but there was no one who would know me.

There was no refuge; no one cared for my soul.
I cried out to You, O LORD. I said,

"You are my refuge and my portion
in the land of the living.

Give attention to my cry,
for I have been brought very low.

Rescue me from my persecutors,
for they are stronger than I.

Bring my soul out of prison,
so that I may praise Your name.

The godly shall be all around me,
for You shall deal bountifully with me."

-Psalm 142

———

"If the psalm prays, you pray; if it laments, you lament;
if it exults, you rejoice; if it hopes, you hope; if it fears, you fear.
Everything written here is a mirror for us."

-St. Augustine (354-430 A.D.)
Monk; Bishop of Hippo, North Africa

8.3 Depression Lifted in Italy, Job in Belgium, Better in India

"Pray, and let God worry."

-Martin Luther (1483-1546)

———

"Therefore do not worry about tomorrow,
for tomorrow will have its own worries.
Today has enough trouble of its own."

-Matthew 6:34

Mar. 3, 2010 - Answer to Prayer:

Dear *Prayer Warriors*, I want to thank first our Heavenly Father for His love, because He answers always the prayers lifted up for the salvation of the souls. I thank also all the Prayer Warriors who have prayed for my daughter Valy. She has come out from her trouble and depression, and last Sunday she goes to Church to worship the Lord. It was two years, she don't come to Church Service. Allelluja! God is good and faithful.

May God bless you all, and give strength and power to your prayers. Love in Jesus, -Aldo (Italy)

———

Mar. 3, 2010 - Answer to Prayer:

Thanking for answered prayer. On January 25, I asked prayer to find a job, being totally without income. I said any odd job was welcome. On February 1st I found a short job, which was said to be for one week, but lasted three weeks. Then I found another Temping job, which started March 1st, and normally lasts six months; possibly longer. I praise the Lord for this!

May the Lord bless abundantly all who prayed!
-Angeline (Brugge, Belgium)

Mar. 7, 2010 - Answer to Prayer:

My 8 1/2 year old son, Allan, as you all know, lacks concentration, is hyper-active, and does not speak in complete sentences like other children his age. I have been sending you prayer requests for Allan's exams and healing. The Lord Jesus Christ had compassion over him, gave Allan concentration to write his exams independently, and showed that He loves and cares for him, by way of the results.

Today Allan's exam results came; he scored 84%, and stood 19th in rank among the 52 children of his class. The Lord has done a wonderful miracle in Allan's life, and I do believe that the day will come when he will be able to speak fully, and concentrate on things. *All thanks and glory to the Lord.*

Thank you all for your prayers for Allan. -Anita (India)

Mar. 31, 2010 - Answer to Prayer:

Thank you so much for your prayers for my Mother. God has answered. Things look better now than they have in a very long time. Sometimes He might not answer when we expect, or in our timing, but He always answers right on time. Thank You, Lord! Hallelujah! Thanks again for all of your prayers.

God bless you all through Christ Jesus Our Lord! -Brandie (Ohio)

Apr. 12, 2010 - Answer to Prayer:

Thank you for your intercessions, as I approach the end of my Town Pastor training. There has been an almost overwhelming amount of difficulty thrown my way through the duration of the course, and even up to the last hours before my first shift.

The training has been successfully completed, as well as the first night of ministry, and subsequent progress interview with the coordinators. I am now in the probationary stage of training, until June / July.

-Brother Bruce (U.K.) 2 Timothy 4:1-5

S.G. Preston

Aug. 12, 2010 - Answer to Prayer:

Greetings in the name of our Lord Most High, to Lay Monk Preston, Lay Monk Linda, and all the other Lay Monks in Portland. We are doing good here, baby Hannah is 2 months old now.

Thanks to all the Lay Monks and family of the *PrayerFoundation*,™ who prayed for Hannah's safe birth. We could feel God's hand and the waves of prayers by the faithful.

Thanks and regards,   -Lay Monk Justin (Wellington, New Zealand)

Dec. 22, 2010 - Answer to Prayer:

Dear *Prayer Warriors*, My husband and I have recently reconciled, after a 4 year separation.

In Christ, -Becky (Massachusetts)

Dec. 25, 2010 - Answer to Prayer:

Dear Brethren, Thank you for joining in prayer for 10 year-old Hannah. She had a very serious heart condition, which the surgeons were uncertain how to treat. She has had an operation, and received a pacemaker.

She is back home with her family now, and it is making all the difference. -Brother Bruce (U.K.)

Dec. 31, 2010 - Answer to Prayer:

I sent a request, I believe nearly a year ago, about a grave misunderstanding that had tremendous implications for me and my family. Today the prayers were answered. God has granted us the deliverance we sought; in kindness, mercy and love. Truth has set us free.

My faith is restored in God's healing love. -(Canada)

Jan. 17, 2011 – Prayer Request:

Please pray for Lay Monk Bob, who has had a cold / flu for four months straight now; with no medicine, including Penicillin, having any effect.

Answer to Prayer - Jan. 25, 2011 (Eight Days Later.)

Thank you for praying for our own Lay Monk Bob (85 years old). God has totally healed him from the severe sickness that he had.

St. Augustine of Hippo (354-430 A.D.) On the Psalms

"Then let the trees of the forest sing, before the arrival of the Lord, who returns to judge the nations, to set the earth aright, restoring the world to order."

-Psalm 96:15

"Our whole purpose is, when we hear a psalm...having been written before our Lord Jesus Christ came in the flesh; to see Christ there, to understand Christ there."

"For the voice (of the Psalms) *is that sweet voice, so well-known to the church; the voice of our Lord Jesus Christ... What utterances I sent up to you, my God, when I read the Psalms of David; those faithful songs and sounds of devotion which exclude all swelling of spirit; ...when new to your true love.*

What utterances I used to send up to you in those psalms, and how I was inflamed towards you by them, and burned to proclaim them, if possible, throughout the whole world, against the pride of the human race!

...I read the fourth psalm in that time of my leisure -- how that psalm wrought upon me, when I spoke by and for myself before You, out of the private feelings of my soul."

S.G. Preston

A Psalm of David.

My God, my God, why have You forsaken Me?

Why are You so far from helping Me,
and from the words of My groaning?

O my God, I cry in the daytime, but You do not hear;
and in the night, and am not silent.

But You are holy,
O You who inhabit the praises of Israel.

Our ancestors trusted in You.
They trusted, and You delivered them.

They cried out to You, and were delivered.
They trusted in You, and were not disappointed.

But I am a worm, and no man;
an object of scorn, and despised by the people.
All who see Me, mock and revile me.

They shake their heads, saying ,
**"He trusted in the LORD to deliver Him.
Let God deliver Him then, if God delighted in Him."**

But You are He who took Me out of the womb.
You caused me to trust in You,
when I was upon My mother's breasts.

I was cast upon You from the womb.
You are My God, from My mother's belly.

Be not far from Me, for trouble is near,
and there are none to help.

Many bulls have surrounded Me.
Strong bulls of Bashan
have besieged Me all around...

**They divide My clothing among them,
and cast lots for one of my garments.**

-Psalm 22:1-12,18

213

8.4 Justice in Italy, Job in the U.K., Healed in Kentucky

*"When I pray, coincidences happen,
and when I don't, they don't."*

-William Temple (1881-1944)
Archbishop of Canterbury

———

*"Elijah was a man subject to like passions as we are,
and he prayed earnestly that it might not rain:
and it rained not on the earth
by the space of three years and six months.
And he prayed again: and the heaven gave rain,
and the earth brought forth her fruit."*

-James 5:17-18

Jan. 18, 2011 - Answer to Prayer:

Dear *Intercessors*, praise the Lord! On the 14th of January, my family and I were called to Court, to answer about a car accident occurred to my daughter Valy, two years ago. The meeting went well for us. The Court understood that the injured party said many lies, to gain much money from our Insurance Company. I thank you for all the prayers lifted up for us. God is good all the time!

Love in Jesus, -Brother Aldo (Italy)

———

Jan. 27, 2011 - Prayer Request:

Please do pray for blessings on my life. I have had a second interview at ***** and they were very positive, but there has been a delay. Pray that all references are good and clean, and there is no bad word said against me, to jeopardize this position. Pray I hear one way or another, but pray for good news about this job, and for a clean and fresh start. Pray for God's favour, and that He will go before me, and I will be successful today. Pray for blessings on my life so that I can be a blessing to others. In Jesus' name, Amen. -Victoria (U.K.)

214

S.G. Preston

Answer to Prayer - Feb. 19, 2011 (Two Weeks Later.)

Dear Lay Monks, I received an offer at ***** in London, and I am delighted. I am waiting for the security and reference checks to go through successfully, so that I can move onto a fresh and new, and joyful stage of my life. Praise God! I had been so anxious waiting for this, and now I have perfect peace about it.

God bless, -Victoria (U.K.)

Mar. 18, 2011 - Answer to Prayer:

Dear *Prayer Warriors*, I want to thank everyone for all the prayers lifted up for Tim. He is at home and doing well. The Doctor got everything, and it has been sent off for testing, but he says it looks good. Wants to see Tim in three to four months. God is so good!!!!!!!

Love in Jesus, -Brother Aldo (Italy)

A Psalm of David.

Hear my prayer, O LORD;
listen to my supplications.
Answer me in Your faithfulness and righteousness.

Do not enter into judgment with Your servant,
for no one living shall be justified in Your sight.

For the enemy has persecuted my soul;
he has struck my life down to the ground.
He has made me to dwell in darkness,
like those that have been long dead.

Therefore my spirit within me is overwhelmed.
My heart is desolate within me.

I remember the days of old;
I meditate on all Your works.
I focus my mind and think deeply
on the work of Your hands.

-Psalm 143:1-5

8.5 *Prayer Warrior* Comments

I would like to register for the Thursday morning, 5:00 a.m. Pacific time slot. That is 8:00 a.m. here. I have been praying for some of the requests posted on the website, and taking on a regular time commitment seems like the next thing to do.

Anyway, I have enjoyed visiting your Site immensely, especially reading the recent story about *Celtic Baptists!* Thanks for writing back about my joining the *Prayerchain.*

God's grace be upon you, -Brother Seamus (Ontario, Canada)

I have found that being involved with your website and work is very spiritually rewarding. I have tried to make my appointed prayer time, but even when missed have made it up at another time. While praying for others' needs, I find so much similarity between all of us.

In praying for others, I have found faith and strength to meet my own challenges. And knowing that there are people praying for me across this country is also very comforting. I pray that God continues to bless your work and that it spreads across the rest of the country.

Yours with you in prayer, -Crandall

I was looking for a place to submit a prayer request for some family and friends and came across your Site. I have found it to be a blessing and look forward to your E-Newsletter.

Would like to be considered to be a *Prayer Warrior* with you. I love praying for people as well as with them. I love praying.

I look forward to the new things that you are starting; looks like more blessing to me. I thank God for using you to touch many lives, with prayers and smiles.

-Sister I.

S.G. Preston

I read something today for my *Spiritual Theology* class that made me think of the *PrayerFoundation* ™ Order. It is by the theologian Nicolas Cabasilas and is quoted in my professor's book as he found it in Kallistos Ware's book, *"Ways of Prayer and Contemplation."*

"Everyone may continue to exercise their art or profession.

The general may continue to command,
the farmer to till the soil,
the workman to pursue his craft.

No one need desist from his usual employment.

It is not necessary to retire into the desert,
or to eat unaccustomed food, or to dress differently,
or to ruin one's health, or to do anything reckless;
for it is quite possible to practice continual meditation
in one's own home without giving up
any of one's possessions."

-Nicholas Cabasilas (c. 1320-c. 1390)
Eastern Orthodox Lay Theologian
Thessalonica, Byzantine Empire

-(Lay Monk) Brother Adam (Princeton, New Jersey)

I was just searching through the web about prayer (and found your website). What I like best are the different quotations and the works of the whole ministry. To tell you honestly, it's got all the things I like to see and hear. I am a born-again Christian and visit your Site daily. I am so profoundly amazed, that at first, I thought maybe it's not the one I'm looking for; but thank God it is. Thank you very much.

My life has been completely turned around since I joined our prayer group here in Sydney. Thank you very much for your helpful tips about praying. It is so delightful to read all of the inspirational quotations from different great religious Christians, as well as chapters and verses from the Bible, which help me a lot in my daily quest for inspirational prayers.

Before, I was only a regular attendee every Saturday, but after three Saturday fellowships they asked me to join the Choir, which I gladly accepted. From then on, my Christian life has become stronger, until recently they asked me to lead the opening prayer.

Thank you very much, because your prayer teaching has helped me make my prayer more involving.

Praise be to God! -Larry (Sydney, Australia)

I stretch out my hands to You.
My soul thirsts for You, like a dry and thirsty land.

Hear me quickly, O LORD, for my spirit fails.

Do not hide Your face from me,
so that I do not become like those who go down into the pit.

Cause me to hear Your loving kindness in the morning,
for I trust in You.

Cause me to know the path in which I should walk,
for I lift up my soul to You.

Deliver me, O LORD, from my enemies.
I flee to You to hide me.

Teach me to do Your will, for You are my God;
Your Good Spirit shall guide me
to the land of the upright.

Because of Your name, O LORD,
You shall give life to me.

In Your righteousness,
You shall lead my soul out of affliction.

In Your mercy,
You shall completely destroy my enemies.

You shall destroy all those who afflict my soul,
for I am Your servant.

-Psalm 143:6-12

8.6 Christ in Genesis 1:1-3

"All you need to do to learn to pray is to pray."

-Wesley L. Duewel (1916-2016) Missionary to India
President, OMS (*One Mission Society*)

———

"Ignorance of Scripture is ignorance of Christ."

-St. Jerome (347-420 A.D.)

———

"There are many who say, 'Who will show us any good?'
LORD, lift up the light of Your countenance upon us.
You have put gladness in my heart;
more than in the time when their grain and their wine increased.
I will both lay myself down in peace, and sleep.
For only You, LORD, enable me to live in safety."

-Psalm 4:6-8

Thoughts On Receiving Answers to Prayer

Because prayer is communion with God, to grow in prayer, we must abide in and grow in Christ. We will grow in prayer through our practice of praying itself, accompanied by immersion in God's word.

When I was a young Christian in my early twenties, I lived across the street from a very large Conservative Synagogue. Jewish Synagogues generally come in four types: Orthodox, Conservative, Reform, and Messianic.

Orthodox Synagogue services are all Hebrew, Conservative Synagogues are a combination of Hebrew and English, and Reform Synagogues are mostly English. Messianic Synagogues are Christian congregations; Jewish people who attend them may refer to themselves Messianic Jews, Completed Jews, or Hebrew Christians.

I told in my book, *Prayer as a Celtic Lay Monk: Learning from Celtic Christian Prayer,* how when I was attending Bible College, my Professor of Old Testament called himself a *Completed Jew.*

219

Psalms Sung in Hebrew

In a Conservative Synagogue, the Psalms are sung as prayers in Hebrew by the Cantor, a professional singer of the Psalms.

I found this feature of the Service to be quite wonderful: it sounded to me as though an angel were singing the Psalms in Heaven.

In the prayer book the Hebrew was on the left side, and the English translation on the right.

You could read along the Psalm in English at the same time the Cantor was singing it in Hebrew.

One day I went over during the week with a tape recorder and asked the Cantor if he would be so kind as to record Genesis Chapter One in Hebrew for me (I wanted to memorize it in Hebrew).

He said he would be glad to, and did I want the Ashkenazic (German / European Jewish) pronunciation, or the Sephardic (Spanish / Middle Eastern Jewish) pronunciation?

Ashkenazic pronunciation is used in American and most European Synagogues. Sephardic pronunciation is what is used in Israel, so I requested that.

Elohim (God)

Many years later, I was with a Jewish friend and for some reason I no longer remember, quoted Genesis 1:1 in Hebrew, which I had memorized so many years before.

She said, "Just so you know, its pronounced *el-lo-him*, not *eh-lo-heem*."

I explained that I wasn't speaking with the Ashkenazic pronunciation of Hebrew used in American Synagogues, but with the Sephardic pronunciation used in Israel.

I think I must have finally surprised her...silence was not typical of her at all!

Pronounced *bay-ray-sheet* in Israel, *Bereshit* is the first word of the Book of Genesis. It is used as the name of the book in Hebrew.

S.G. Preston

Genesis

The Greek word *Genesis* is the first word in the Greek Septuagint translation of the Old Testament. Of course, it is also used in English Bibles. The first part of Genesis 1:1 in Hebrew transliterates into English letters as:

Bereshit bara Elohim et hashamayim ve'et ha'aretz.

בְּרֵאשִׁית בָּרָא אֱלֹהִים אֵת הַשָּׁמַיִם וְאֵת הָאָרֶץ

(*Note:* the Hebrew is read from right to left.)

בְּרֵאשִׁית *Bereshit* (*in the beginning*)

בָּרָא *bara* (*He created*)

(*Note:* The verb "*He created*" here in Hebrew appears before the noun "*God*;" translated into English, the opposite order is correct.)

אֱלֹהִים *Elohim* (*God*)

הַשָּׁמַיִם *hashamayim* (*the heavens*)

וְאֵת *ve'et* (*and*)

הָאָרֶץ *ha'aretz* (*the earth*)

"*The heavens and the earth.*" is a common Hebrew expression meaning: "*everything.*"

Elohim Bara

Ha'Aretz (*The Earth*) is the name of a well-known Newspaper in Israel.

Elohim is translated using the English word *God* throughout the Old Testament.

It is also used when speaking of false gods, because the plural ending "*im*" is what is used to make words plural in Hebrew, the same way "*s*" is used in English.

Bara is a *singular* verb (*He created*).

So in Hebrew, the mystery of the Trinity is built into one of the names of God, the first one used in Scripture. Literally: *God* (*Elohim* with the "*im*" plural) *He created* (singular verb).

221

The Trinity

In the first three verses of the Bible we see the Trinity also:

God (the Father), The (Holy) Spirit of God,
The Word of God (God said)

(Boldface mine.)
*"In the beginning **God created** the heavens and the earth.*
And the earth was without form and void,
and darkness was upon the face of the deep.
*And **the Spirit of God** moved upon the face of the waters.*
*And **God said**, 'Let there be light.' and there was light."*

-Genesis 1:1-3

New Testament

In the New Testament, the Gospel of John explains:

"In the beginning was the Word, and the Word was with God,
and the Word was God. The same was in the beginning with God.

All things were made through Him,
and without Him was not anything made that was made.

And the Word was made flesh, and dwelt among us; and we beheld
His glory, the glory of the only begotten of the Father;
full of grace and truth."

-John 1:1-3, 14

———

"That one who was from the beginning,
who we have heard, who we have seen with our eyes,
who we have looked upon, and our hands have touched,
of the Word of life;

for the life was manifested, and we have seen, and bear witness, and
show to you that eternal life, who was with the Father, and was
manifested to us..."

-1 John 1:1-2

222

S.G. Preston

Blessed Is He

*"And He was clothed with a robe dipped in blood:
and His name is called The Word of God."*

-Revelation 19:13

———

*"For I say to you, you shall not see Me from this time until you say:
'Blessed is He who arrives in the name of the Lord!'"*

-Matthew 23:39; Luke 13:35; Psalm 118:26

———

Baruch ha shem Adonai!
Blessed is the name of the Lord!

Baruch haba ha shem Adonai!
Blessed is He who arrives in the name of the Lord!

Baruch ha shem ha Mashiach Y'eshua!
Blessed is the name of the Messiah Jesus!

To the Director of Music: on stringed instruments.
A Psalm of David.

Hear me when I call, O God of my righteousness.
You have set me free, when I was in distress.
Have mercy on me, and hear my prayer.

You children of humanity,
how long will you turn My glory into shame?
How long will you love delusions, and seek after lies? Selah.

But know that the LORD has set apart for Himself the Holy One;
therefore the LORD will hear me, when I call to Him.

Be angry, but do not sin.
Meditate in your heart on Your bed, and be still. Selah.

Offer the sacrifices of righteousness,
and put your trust in the LORD.

-Psalm 4:1-5

8.7 Christ With Abraham

"Before Abraham was born, I AM."

-John 8:48

———

*"After these things the word of the LORD
came to Abram in a vision:*

*'Fear not, Abram: I am your shield,
and your exceedingly great reward.'"*

-Genesis 15:1

———

*"Listen to Me, you that follow after righteousness;
you that seek the LORD:*

*Look to the rock from which you were carved,
and to the hole of the pit from which you were dug.*

*Look to Abraham your father, and to Sarah who bore you;
for I called him alone, and blessed him, and increased him."*

-Isaiah 51:1-2

———

*"And Abraham believed in the LORD,
and God counted it to him for righteousness."*

-Genesis 15:6; Romans 4:3,9,22;
Galatians 3:6; James 2:23

Theophany

The more we learn about Christ through the Holy Scriptures, and commune with the Father through Christ by the Holy Spirit, the deeper our prayer life will be, for the definition of prayer is communion with God. In the Old Testament, *Theophanies* are appearances of God to men. Abraham was visited by God (the pre-incarnate Christ) and two angels, all three in human form.

S.G. Preston

Seeing God Face to Face

"And the LORD appeared to him (Abraham) in the plains of Mamre,
as he sat in the tent door in the heat of the day."

-Genesis 18:1

Jacob wrestled with an "angel" (it was God, the pre-incarnate
Christ):

"And Jacob called the name of the place Peniel,
'For I have seen God face to face, and my life is preserved.'"

-Genesis 32:30

Moses heard God speak from the burning bush, watched the finger
of God write the Ten Commandments in stone, and God allowed
Moses to see His back as He walked by:

"And the LORD descended in the cloud, and stood with him there...
And the LORD passed by before him..."

-Exodus 34:5-6

"And the LORD spoke to Moses face to face,
as a man speaks to his friend."

-Exodus 33:11

Pre-Incarnate Christ

Joshua saw the Captain of the Lord's Armies (the great Hosts of
angels). Joshua worshipped Him and was not stopped, proving it
was not an angel, but God. The *angels* (meaning: *messengers*) that
appear in scripture never allow themselves to be worshipped.

"'...as Captain of the Armies of the LORD, I have arrived.'

And Joshua fell on his face to the earth,
and worshipped Him, and said to Him,

'What does my Lord say to His servant?'"

-Joshua 5:14

Lord, Show Us the Father

A fourth "man" (*"...like the Son of God."* -Daniel 3:25) appeared in the fiery furnace with Shadrach, Meshach, and Abednego. Theophanies of the pre-incarnate Christ are referred to as *Christophanies*.

During His Incarnation, tens of thousands of people saw God: that is, they saw *Christ, the Second Person of the Trinity, God the Son.* In the New Testament, at times when just the word *God* is used, the context shows it to be referring to the First Person of the Trinity: *God the Father.* The Bible states that no one has ever seen God the Father:

"No one at any time has seen God.

***The only begotten Son, who is Himself God,
and is in the closest relationship with the Father,
He has revealed Him."***

-John 1:18

———

"If you had known Me, you should have known My Father also; from this time forward you both know Him, and have seen Him.

*Philip said to Him,
"Lord, show us the Father, and it is sufficient for us."
Jesus said to Him, "Have I been so long with you,
and yet you have not known Me, Philip?
He that has seen Me has seen the Father.*

*Why do you say then, 'Show us the Father?'
Do you not believe that I am in the Father,
and the Father in Me?"*

-John 14:7-10

———

"I and My Father are one."

-John 10:30

226

S.G. Preston

Tetragrammaton

At the burning bush, Moses asked God His name, and heard God's voice speak the *Tetragrammaton*, the four Hebrew letters of God's holy name (YHWH יהוה).   According to the 1906 *Jewish Encyclopedia,* it is used in the Old Testament 5,410 times:

"And God said to Moses,
I AM THAT I AM';

and He said,
This you shall say to the sons of Israel:
'I AM' (YHWH יהוה) *has sent me to you..."*

"...this is My name forever,
and this is My memorial to all generations."

-Exodus 3:14-15

In Hebrew, JHVH, with the "J" having a "Y" sound (as in the Scandinavian languages) and the "V" having a "W" sound (the exact opposite of German); therefore in English it is correctly translated as: YHWH.

This is why the King James Version's *Jehovah* is a totally *impossible* pronunciation, and why the Jerusalem Bible (and some other versions) use *Yahweh* instead.

Hallelu-Yah

There is absolutely no way to know how to pronounce the second syllable, because ancient Hebrew has no vowels. However, the first syllable is definitely *Yah,* because we have the word *halleluyah* (meaning: *praise God*). We know that the Hebrew word *hallelu* by itself means *praise.*

The Jewish people felt that this name of God was too holy to ever speak, so they never spoke it. Instead they said *Adonai* (*Lord*) whenever they came to it in Scripture.

Some Jewish people today prefer to say *ha-Shem* (*the Name*).

227

The LORD

Never having been pronounced for thousands of years, today the actual correct pronunciation of the vowel for the second syllable (WH) is no longer known.

In most English Bibles where the *Tetragrammaton* appears, the words *the LORD, with LORD* written in all capital letters, will be found in its place. This is how we know that God appeared to Abraham in human form, as recorded in Genesis 18:1...

"And the LORD appeared to him in the plains of Mamre
as he sat in the tent door in the heat of the day.

He lifted up his eyes and looked,
and lo, three men stood before him.

When he saw them, he ran to meet them from the tent door,
and bowed himself toward the ground..."

-Genesis 18:1-2

We also know that the other two "men" were *angels* because:

"And the men turned away from there,
and went toward Sodom;
but Abraham stood yet
before the LORD."

"And two angels arrived in Sodom at evening,
as Lot was sitting in the gate of Sodom."

-Genesis 18:22, 19:1

We next learn that Abraham was aware that he was speaking to God:

"And Abraham answered, saying,
'Behold now, I have taken upon me
to speak to the LORD,
who am but dust and ashes..."

-Genesis 18:27

S.G. Preston

From the LORD Out of Heaven

Abraham's conversation with God about how many righteous men needed to be in Sodom for it not to be destroyed, was not done through prayer, as I had always mistakenly thought.

It was an actual face to face conversation with God in human form, the pre-incarnate Christ:

> *"And the LORD went his way,*
> *as soon as He had finished talking with Abraham,*
> *and Abraham returned to his place."*

> -Genesis 18:33

We know what happened with the angels in Sodom: they couldn't find ten righteous men there, and so they pulled Lot out of the city (Genesis 19:1-23).

The very next verse informs us:

> *"Then the LORD rained upon Sodom and upon Gomorrah brimstone*
> *and fire from the LORD out of heaven."*

> -Genesis 19:24

Here we have another example from Holy Scripture of the Trinity in the Old Testament (or at least two-thirds of the Trinity!). This is a truly amazing verse of Holy Scripture:

> *"Then the LORD God Yahweh* יהוה (on the Earth)
> rained down upon Sodom and Gomorrah brimstone and fire
> from *the LORD God Yahweh* יהוה *out of heaven."*

Prayer Tip: If you would like to begin adding the praying of Psalms to your daily prayer time (like Jesus, the Apostles, and the many great prayer Christians quoted in this book), most Christians will begin by memorizing the 23rd Psalm (the *King James Version* is the one most commonly memorized). Enjoy! God bless!

229

8.8 Answer to Prayer: Israel & Jerusalem

Answer to Prayer: Israel

Prayer Request (September 8, 70 A.D. - May 13, 1948)

By the Jewish people to return to Israel and its becoming a Nation again, as their Jewish Homeland.

In 70 A.D. the Roman General Titus (later Roman Emperor) put down the Jewish rebellion against Rome after a siege of Jerusalem. The Jewish Temple was destroyed. In 135 A.D. the Romans combined the two provinces of Syria and Judaea and renamed the new province: Syria Palestrina (Palestine). Many of the Jewish people were relocated to other areas of the Roman Empire.

Answer to Prayer - May 14, 1948 (978 Years Later.)

The Prophet Ezekiel lived c. 622-c. 570 B.C. From datable information found in the text of the Book of Ezekiel itself, Ezekiel's prophecies were given over the course of approximately 22 years, the last given in 570 B.C. This is the prophecy in the Bible (Ezekiel 11:17), of the return of the Jewish people to the land of Israel, and of God's return of the *Land of Israel* to the Jewish people:

"Therefore say, 'Thus says the LORD God:
'I will even gather you from the people, and assemble you out of the countries where you have been scattered,
and I will give you the land of Israel (Eretz Yisrael אֶרֶץ יִשְׂרָאֵל)."

Prophecy Fulfilled May 14, 1948

The United Nations voted to end British Mandate control over Palestine, and proposed a Partition into Jewish and Palestinian areas. On May 14, 1948, David Ben-Gurion, the head of the *Jewish Agency*, accepted the UN's Partition proposal, and proclaimed the establishment of the State of Israel.

Both the U.S. President Harry S. Truman, and the Soviet Union's Joseph Stalin, formally recognized the new nation on that same day.

S.G. Preston

Answer to Prayer: Jerusalem

Prayer Request: - (September 8, 70 A.D. - June 9, 1967)
For nearly 2,000 Years at every Passover Seder:

"Next Year in Jerusalem!"

The siege of Jerusalem lasted from April 14 - September 8 (4 months, 3 weeks, and 4 days). Destruction of Jerusalem and the Temple occurred on September 8, 70 A.D. This was prophesied by Christ in the New Testament:

"And as some spoke of the Temple, how it was adorned with beautiful stones and gifts, He said, 'As for these things which you are seeing, the days will arrive, in which there will not be one stone left upon another, that shall not be thrown down.'

And they asked Him, saying, 'Teacher, but when shall these things take place? And what sign will there be when these things shall occur?' 'When you shall see Jerusalem surrounded by armies, then know that its destruction is near.'"

-Luke 21:5-7, 20

According to Christ in the New Testament, *"the times of the Gentiles"* would begin in 70 A.D., with the prophesied destruction of Jerusalem and the Temple; and would end with the return of Jerusalem to Jewish control.

Answer to Prayer - June 10, 1967 (1,897 Years Later.)

After nearly 2,000 years of possession by Gentiles, on June 10, 1967 during the *Six Day War*, Israel took control of the Temple Mount and the Old City of Jerusalem, fulfilling this prophecy of Christ:

"Jerusalem shall be trodden down by the Gentiles, until the times of the Gentiles are fulfilled."

-Luke: 21:24

But our prayers are still needed:

"Pray for the peace of Jerusalem. They shall prosper that love you."

-Psalm 122:6

* * *

231

8.9 Lay Monk Thoughts: Answers to Prayer

"Ma's math leat sìth, càirdeas, agus cluain --
éisd, faic, 'us fuirich sàmhach."

"If you wish peace, friendship, and quietness:
listen, look, and be silent."

-Old Gaelic Saying

———

"My meditation of Him shall be sweet:
I will be glad in the LORD."

-Psalm 104:34

Jan. 23, 2002 - Prayer Request:

My 27 year-old son, Trent, living hand-to-mouth in L.A. has been on and off "speed" (mostly on) for 9 years. Please pray that Trent will be delivered permanently from drugs, healed of his psychological wounds, and above all that he will surrender his life in service to Jesus Christ.

Thank you, and may God mightily bless your prayer ministry.

-Rick

Additional Prayer Request - Apr. 15, 2002 (6 Weeks Later.)

My son Trent has a court appearance on Wednesday, April 17. Please pray that God will grant him extreme favor and leniency in the disposition of his case.

Thank you for your prayers. -Rick

Answer to Prayer - Apr. 17, 2002 (Two Days Later.)

Thank you for praying for my son, Trent. He did, indeed, receive a very favorable ruling today! Last night he was reading the Bible, and two other inmates joined him in an impromptu study and prayer session.

-Rick

Additional Prayer Request, and an Answer to Prayer Update - Apr. 24, 2002 (One Week Later.)

My son Trent has another court appearance tomorrow. Please pray that the judge will release Trent immediately. Yes, Trent has received blessings and insights from God while in jail. He says: "I want to come home and start to jog every day, and eat right, and heal my body, and go to Bible studies at night."

Thank you for your prayers. -Rick

Answer to Prayer - 2nd Update - Apr. 26, 2002 (Two Days Later.)

Thank you for your prayers. My son, Trent, is home with us! Praise the Lord!

Over the past three weeks, Trent has been the recipient of many miraculous blessings. Today, God intervened again and Trent was released from jail.

He still has a few court appearances which will determine the level and length of mandated rehab. I'll keep you posted.

Thanks again, and God bless you! -Rick

Answer to Prayer - 3rd Update

Your continued prayers for my son, Trent, are working! Praise God! He continues to grow and change in the Lord!

Trent studies the Word on his own, tirelessly. He's doing an in-depth study workbook for Romans.

He's active in a Spirit-filled church, and this Sunday will be serving in the Children's Church. He demonstrates *no* interest in the worldly music or entertainment that used to enthrall him. Now, it's only Jesus!

Also, he's quit smoking cigarettes! Satan often gnaws at Trent with drug-related memories, but he has learned to "pray through" these times.

Thanks again, -Rick

Email from Trent - Received Apr. 26, 2002
Nine Years On "Speed" Ended and Received Christ
(Two and a Half Months After Initial Prayer Request.)

Hello friends, Wow! Freedom! It sure is a good thing. Having developed a personal relationship with Jesus about 2 & 1/2 weeks ago is even better.

The love and peace I feel is like nothing that the world could give to me. Thank you all so much for your many prayers. They worked! I just want to jump and shout for joy. In jail, I began reading the book of John. Awesome stuff!

I am so excited about my new life, and I'm so lucky my dad is a true man of God. I asked him if he will baptize me sometime next week, either in his swimming pool or at the beach.

What a relief, I can leave the past behind. Amen. -Trent

Oct. 24, 2007 - Answer to Prayer (Two Weeks Later.)
Received Three Years Later.

About three years ago, I found your website and sent in a prayer request for prayer for myself.

For the previous two years, I had been suffering from what I believed was an infection in my body, as well as back trouble that I had for many years.

Within a few weeks of sending in my prayer request I received, through unusual circumstances, an incredible healing.

-Gary (Louisville, Kentucky)

Apr. 26, 2011 - Answer to Prayer (Two Weeks Later.)
Updated: Six Years and Three Months Later.

On your website under *Answers to Prayer* on the date 10/24/07, you will see my name, and a previously answered prayer. It starts out:

"About three years ago I found your website..."

234

Today, about 39 months from that date, I'm visiting your website again, I believe led here by God. Suddenly, today out of the blue, I remembered your website. I knew I had requested prayer from you...

My problem was, I couldn't remember the name of your website. I just typed in *prayer website*. After scrolling through 29 pages of prayer-related websites, I found your website on page 30 of my *Yahoo* search. I was very excited.

I was healed two weeks after I asked you for prayer. I apparently had not sent you any information about what had happened (my healing), until three years later.

I had back problems for years, and was completely healed two weeks later.

Thank you for all your previous prayers, and for all the prayers you've sent out for everyone else, and thank God for all those answered prayers and miracles, which bring hope and faith to us all.

-Gary (Louisville, Kentucky)

Draw Near to God, and He Will Draw Near to You (James 4:8)

*"The Lord is near to all who call upon Him,
to all who call upon Him in truth."*

-Psalm 145:18

Answers to Prayer

Rick and his son Trent's emails to us in 2002, and Gary's emails to us from 2007 and 2011, are the ones with which I have chosen to end this book.

But of course for us, the *Answers to Prayer* have continued daily, up to the re-writing, compiling, and editing of this book in 2021.

They tell authors never to repeat anything in a book. But they also tell teachers to always repeat your main point three times! I therefore will go ahead and repeat here two of my all-time favorite prayer quotes, that you have already seen on the Title Page of this book.

And the Answers Are Always Coming

It is my prayer for you that they will be as much of a blessing and inspiration to you throughout your life, as they have been to me in mine:

"I live in the spirit of prayer.
I pray as I walk about, when I lie down, and when I rise up.
And the answers are always coming."

-George Müller (1805-1898) Best book about:
George Müller: Delighted in God by Roger Steer

The Story of Your Life

"As white snowflakes fall quietly
and thickly on a winter day,
answers to prayer
will settle down upon you
at every step you take,
even to your dying day.

The story of your life
will be the story of prayer,
and answers to prayer."

-O. Hallesby (1879-1961)
Author of the book: *Prayer*

* * * * *

S.G. Preston

If You Have Been Blessed In Any Way, By Anything In This Book

Or have just enjoyed it, would you please be so kind as to leave a Review for this book at *Amazon Books?* Just Google: *Answers to Prayer* and click on the Book Cover. The place to leave a Review is near the bottom of the page.

Thank you so much, and may God continue to richly bless you as you serve Him!

If You Would Like to *Subscribe* to our *PrayerFoundation Evangelical Lay Monks* ™ (prayerfoundation.net) E-Newsletter, just send the word...

Subscribe to: monks@prayerfoundation.org

———

Now That You Have Read this Book

We recommend using it like a Daily Devotional. Place it on your nightstand and read a page or two each day.

You will be blessed by reading and re-reading inspiring teaching from some of the *Greatest Lives of Prayer* of the past three thousand years:

"...keep the clean sea breeze of the centuries blowing through our minds..."

-C.S. Lewis (1898-1963)
Author: *Mere Christianity*

* * *

About the Author

S.G. Preston and his wife Linda, Evangelical Protestants, founded the *PrayerFoundation* ™ and its associated Lay Monastic Order, the *Knights of Prayer* ™ in 1999. It was the first Evangelical Monastic Order on the Internet, and remained the only one for the next four years. They live in the beautiful Pacific Northwest with four cats and a Scottish Terrier named Hermiston, where they enjoy prayer and Bible study, attending Church, hiking (with Hermiston), camping, canoeing, cycling, sailing, skiing, and horseback riding.

S.G. Preston Ministries ™

(List of Ministries and Contact Information):

Email: monks@prayerfoundation.org

The Prayer Foundation (Founded 1999) *PrayerFoundation* ™
International, Interdenominational, Evangelical.

Original Website: www.prayerfoundation.org (went Online 1999)
The Prayer Foundation
Over 1,300 Webpages of *"Prayer Teaching and Resources from All Christian Communions and Eras."*
New Website: www.prayerfoundation.net
PrayerFoundation Lay Monks ™ (went Online 2020).

E-Newsletter (Monthly): send the word *Subscribe* to...
monks@prayerfoundation.org

Knights of Prayer Lay Monks ™ (Founded 1999).
Married or Single, remaining in their own jobs, careers, churches.
Lay Monks have joined from all 50 U.S. States and 47 Countries worldwide.

Publishing: *PrayerFoundation Press* ™ (Founded 2018).

Recommended Ministry:

Redeem TV Streaming Goodness. (Our Favorite TV Channel!)

(Christian Film Streaming Service founded by Bill Curtis, President of *Vision Video / Christian History Institute*.

"A donor-supported, ad-free, streaming service with no fees. Our goal is to provide edifying and redemptive visual media content for all ages."

redeemtv.com   watch.redeemtv.com

Christian History Magazine (Our Favorite Magazine!)

Published four times per year, and available by donation through the *Christian History Institute* ministry. We have subscribed for over a decade and have collected back issues of all but four of the over 125 past issues. It is always exciting to receive each new issue!

christianhistoryinstitute.org

S.G. Preston

Recommended Books:

In Bold: Must Read (or: **Must Listen To** on Audiobook if available).
In Italics: Highly Recommended
Not in Italics: Recommended.

Prayer:

"Power Through Prayer" by E.M. Bounds

"The Kneeling Christian" (Anonymous)

"Hudson Taylor's Spiritual Secret" by Dr. Taylor

"George Muller: Delighted in God" by Roger Steer

"The Practice of the Presence of God" by Brother Lawrence

"Prayer" by O. Hallesby

"Psalms: The Prayer Book of the Bible" by Dietrich Bonhoeffer

(All other books on prayer by E.M. Bounds)

"The Path of Celtic Prayer" by Calvin Miller

"The Path of Prayer" by Samuel Chadwick

"The Power of Prayer" by R.A. Torrey

"With Christ in the School of Prayer" by Andrew Murray

"The Life and Diary of David Brainerd" Edited by Jonathan Edwards (Scholarly)

Basic Christian Teaching:

"Mere Christianity" by C.S. Lewis

"Knowing God" by J.I. Packer

"Growing in Christ" by J.I. Packer

"God Wrote a Book" by James McDonald

"Spiritual Disciplines for the Christian Life" by Donald S. Whitney

"Christ, Baptism and the Lord's Supper: Recovering the Sacraments for Evangelicals" by Leonard Vander Zee

"The Confessions" by St. Augustine

"On the Incarnation" by St. Athanasius of Alexandria (Scholarly)

"The Knowledge of the Holy" by A.W. Tozer

Christian Life:

"L'Abri" **by Edith Schaeffer** (Autobiography)

"Desiring God" **by John Piper** (Teaching)

"E.M. Bounds: Man of Prayer" **by Lyle Dorsett** (Biography)

"Don't Waste Your Life" by John Piper (Teaching)

"Spurgeon On Leadership" by Larry J. Michael

"St. Francis of Assisi" by Omer Englebert (Biography)

Daily Devotional:

"The Imitation of Christ" by Thomas à Kempis

Celtic Christianity / Celtic Monasticism:

"How the Irish Saved Civilization" **by Thomas Cahill** (second half of book only, from *St. Patrick* on: History of Irish Celtic Monasticism) (Note: This is a book written by a Secular Author)

"Sun Dancing" **by Geoffrey Moorhouse** (History of Monks at Skellig Michael) (Note: This is a book written by a Secular Author)

"Celtic Christianity: Yesterday, Today, and for the Future" by Paul D.J. Arblaster

"Flame in My Heart: St Aidan for Today" by David Adam

"The Path of Celtic Prayer" by Calvin Miller

"Thin Places: An Evangelical Journey into Celtic Christianity" by Tracy Balzer

"The Celtic Way of Evangelism" by George G. Hunter III

S.G. Preston

Early Church Teaching and Practice:

"Reading Scripture with the Church Fathers" by Christopher A. Hall

"Learning Theology with the Church Fathers" by Christopher A. Hall

"Worshipping with the Church Fathers" by Christopher A. Hall

"Living Wisely with the Church Fathers" by Christopher A. Hall

"Ancient-Future Faith" by Robert E. Webber

"Ancient-Future Worship" by Robert E. Webber

"Ancient-Future Time" by Robert E. Webber

"The Sign of the Cross: The Gesture, the Mystery, the History" by Andreas Andreopoulos

"Getting to Know the Church Fathers: An Evangelical Introduction" by Bryan Litfin

"Beyond Smells and Bells: The Wonder and Power of Christian Liturgy" by Mark Galli

"A New Song for an Old World: Musical Thought in the Early Church" by Calvin R. Stapert

"Evangelicals and Nicene Faith: Reclaiming the Apostolic Witness" Editor: Timothy George

"Retrieving the Tradition & Renewing Evangelicalism: A Primer for Suspicious Protestants" by D.H. Williams (Perhaps a little too basic for most Evangelical Lay Monks – perfect to give to the skeptical!)

Christian History:

"Here I Stand: A Life of Martin Luther" by Roland Bainton

"Church History in Plain Language" by Bruce L. Shelley

"History of the Christian Church," Volumes 1-6 by Philip Schaff

"The Ecclesiastical History of the English People" by the Venerable Bede (Only the section on the ancient Celtic Monks; Scholarly)

"The History of the Church: From Christ to Constantine" by Eusebius (Scholarly)

243

Note: The books directly below are some of my all-time favorite books. I've read them three times each (so far) but I realize that they are not for everyone. *If* you are a Christian who *loves the History of Christian Doctrine and Liturgy,* they are **must read**:

"Credo" **by Jaroslav Pelikan** (Scholarly)

"The Christian Tradition," **Volumes 1-5, by Jaroslav Pelikan** (Scholarly)

"The Shape of the Liturgy" **by Dom Gregory Dix** (Scholarly)

Apologetics:

"I Don't Have Enough Faith to Be an Atheist" by Norman L. Geisler and Frank Turek

Excellent Audio Bibles:

Word of Promise **(Dramatic Audio Theater:** *New King James Version***)** Old and New Testament (Available separately or together). Read by Innumerable Top Actors and Actresses – listens like a Movie Soundtrack. Thomas Nelson Publishers. Our favorite!

New Testament **Read by Johnny Cash** (*New King James Version*).

Holy Bible **NIV Read by David Suchet** (Complete Bible: New International Version) (Suchet played: *Hercule Poirot* in the Television Series).

Excellent Audio Bible Commentary:

Thru the Bible Radio: **Dr. J. Vernon McGee** (Commentary on the Entire Bible) 5-Year Radio Program: listen daily on Christian AM Radio. Also available on CD or MP3. I've listened to the entire Commentary at least 6 times and look forward to listening to Dr. McGee off and on for life! Also available in Book form, which we also have (the transcribed Radio talks), for reading or for reference use. (www.ttb.org)

S.G. Preston

Recommended Films:

Key: **(In Bold) Must See.**
(*In Italics*) *Highly Recommended.*

Full-Length Films:

"Brother Sun, Sister Moon" by Franco Zefirelli (early ministry of St. Francis) (Our favorite Film of all time!)

"The Nativity Story" (Keisha Castle-Hughes)

"Esther" (Bible Collection: F. Murray Abraham, Louise Lombard) (Made for TV: 1 Hr.)

"Luther" (Joseph Fiennes)

"St. Patrick: The Irish Legend" (Patrick Bergin, Malcolm McDowell). Excellent! But some may not like that fictional "Legendary" stories are also included.

"Hudson Taylor"

"The Gospel of John" (Word for Word: *Good News Bible*) The Film is fantastic! (The additional Commentary at the end is worthless: we recommend not watching it).

Docudramas:

"Martin Luther" (PBS)

"St. Patrick: Apostle of Ireland" (includes the complete actual words of St. Patrick)

"Robber of the Cruel Streets" (About George Müller)

Documentaries:

"A History of Christian Worship: Ancient Ways, Future Paths" (6 DVDs)
"History of Christianity" (6 Parts on 2 DVDs) by Dr. Timothy George

Celtic Christian:

"My Journey to Life: On the Trail of Celtic Saints" by Rainer Walde
"Blessing Europe: The Legacy of the Celtic Saints" by Rainer Walde

Bibliography:

Primary Sources:

Acts of the Martyrdom of Saint Justin and His Companions (earlyChristians.org)

Adomnan of Iona, St.; *Life of St. Columba* (Penguin Books, 1995)

à Kempis, Thomas; *The Imitation of Christ* (Random House, 1998)

Athanasius, St.; *On the Incarnation*; (St. Vladimir's Seminary Press, 2003)

Athanasius, St.; *Life of Antony* (Ancient Christian Writer's Series; Paulist Press, 1950)

Augustine, St.; *The City of God* (Hendrickson Publishing, 2009)

Augustine, St.; *The Confessions* (Barnes & Noble, 2007)

Augustine, St.; *Epistle to Januarius* (Letter 53, Chapter 2); Fathers; (New Advent, 2020)

Benedict, St.; *The Rule of St. Benedict* (Random House, 1998)

Bede, St.; The Venerable; *The Ecclesiastical History of the English People* (Translated by Leo Sherley-Price; Penguin Books, 1990)

Bede, St., The Venerable; *The Life and Miracles of St. Cuthbert, Bishop of Lindisfarne* (Internet History Sourcebook Project; Fordham University)

Basil the Great, St.; *The Hexameron* (CreateSpace Publishing, 2014)

Basil the Great, St.; *Monastic Rule of St. Basil the Great* (Athletis Publishing, 2018)

Bonhoeffer, Dietrich; *The Cost of Discipleship* (Touchstone, 1995)

Bonhoeffer, Dietrich; *Psalms: The Prayer Book of the Bible* (Augsburg, 1970)

Bounds, E.M.; *Power Through Prayer* (Destiny Image, 2007)

Bounds, E.M.; *The Complete Works of E.M. Bounds On Prayer* (Baker Books, 1990)

Brainerd, David; *The Life and Diary of David Brainerd*; Edited by Jonathan Edwards (Baker Books, 1989)

Brother Lawrence; *The Practice of the Presence of God* (Baker Books, 1989)

Cassian, John; *The Conferences* (Translated by Boniface Ramsay, O.P.; Newman Press, 1997)

Cassian, John; *The Institutes* (Translated by Boniface Ramsay, O.P.; Newman Press, 2000)

Catholic Encyclopedia, The; Pope Honorius I, Entry by J. Chapman; New York: Robert Appleton Company, 1910)

Climacus, John; *The Ladder of Divine Ascent* (Paulist Press, 1982)

Davies, Oliver; Translator, *Celtic Spirituality* (Paulist Press, 1999)

Didache, or The Teaching of the Twelve Apostles (Translated by James A. Kleist, S.J., Ph.D.; Newman Press, 1948)

Eusebius; *The History of the Church: From Christ to Constantine* (Penguin Books, 1989)

Foxe, John; *Foxe's Book of Martyrs* (Bridge-Logos, 2001)

Henry, Matthew; *Exposition of the Old and New Testaments*, 6 Vol. (Nabu Press, 2011)

Hippolytus; *On the Apostolic Tradition* (St. Vladimir's Seminary Press, 2001)

Irenaeus of Lyon, St.; *Against Heresies,* Books 1-3 (Paulist Press, 2012)

Jewish Encyclopedia, The: A Descriptive Record of the History, Religion, Literature and Custom of the Jewish People; 12 Vol. (Isidore Singer, Editor; January 1, 1906)

Josephus, Flavius; *The Life* (CreateSpace, 2013)

Lewis, C.S.; *Fern-seed and Elephants and Other Essays On Christianity*; Essay: *Modern Theology and Biblical Criticism* (Fontana, 1975)

Lewis, C.S.; *Letters to Malcolm: Chiefly On Prayer* (HarperCollins, 1984)

Lewis, C.S.; *Mere Christianity* (HarperCollins, 1996)

Luther, Martin; *Luther's Small Catechism* (Concordia, 2017)

Moody, Dwight; *Prevailing Prayer* (Aneko Press, 2018)

Murray, Andrew; *With Christ in the School of Prayer* (Classic Reprint, 2017)

Norris, Kathleen; *Dakota: A Spiritual Geography* (Mariner Books, 2001)

O'Maiden, Uinsean, OCR (Translator), *The Celtic Monk: Rules and Writings of Early Irish Monks* (Cistercian Publications, 1996)

Oxford English Dictionary (Oxford University Press, 2012)

Packer, J.I.; *Growing In Christ* (Crossway Books, 2007)

Packer, J.I.; *Knowing God* (InterVarsity Press, 1973)

Palladius, *The Lausiac History* (Ancient Christian Writers Series, No. 34; Paulist Press, 1965)

Patrick of Ireland, St.; *The Works of St. Patrick* (Ancient Christian Writers Series, No. 17; Paulist Press, 1953)

Piper, John; *Desiring God*; (Revised Edition; Multnomah, 2011)

Piper, John; *Don't Waste Your Life* (Crossway, 1994)

Service Books of the Orthodox Church (St. Tikhon's Monastic Press, 2013)

    The Divine Liturgy of St. Basil the Great

    The Divine Liturgy of St. John Chrysostom

Shakespeare, William; *Romeo & Juliet* (Sparknotes, 2019)

Spurgeon, Charles; *Spiritual Warfare In A Believer's Life* (YWAM Publishing, 1996)

Spurgeon, Charles; *The Treasury of David*; (Commentary on the Psalms; Updated Edition in Today's Language; Thomas Nelson, 1997)

Tertullian, *The Chaplet, or De Corona* (Lighthouse Publishing, 2015)

Tertullian (Translator: Greek to Latin), *The Passion of Saints Perpetua and Felicity* (Medieval Sourcebook, Fordham University)

Tertullian, *On Prayer* (Kessinger Publishing, 2015)

Thoreau, Henry David; *Walden: or, Life in the Woods* (Houghton Mifflin, 2004)

Tolkien, J.R.R.; *The Lord of the Rings* (Mariner Books, 2012)

Tolkien, J.R.R.; *Tree and Leaf* (HarperCollins, 2001)

Torrey, R. A.; *The Power of Prayer* (Zondervan, 1971)

Tozer, A.W.; *The Knowledge of the Holy* (HarperCollins, 1961)

Vincent of Lérins, St.; *The Commonitory of St. Vincent of Lerins*; Paul A. Boer Sr. Editor (Veritatis Splendor Publications, 2012)

S.G. Preston

Secondary Sources:

Adam, David; *Fire of the North: The Illustrated life of St. Cuthbert* (SPCK, 1993)

Adam, David; *Flame in My Heart: St. Aidan for Today* (Morehouse Publishing, 1998)

Andreopoulos, Andreas; *The Sign of the Cross: The Gesture, the Mystery, the History* (Paraclete Press, 2006)

Arblaster, Paul D.J.; *Celtic Christianity: Yesterday, Today, and for the Future* (Virtualbookworm.com, 2002)

Bitel, Lisa M.; *Isle of the Saints: Monastic Settlement and Christian Community in Early Ireland* (Cornell University Press, 1990)

Bainton, Roland; *Here I Stand; A Life of Martin Luther* (Penguin Books, 1995)

Cahill, Thomas; *How the Irish Saved Civilization* (Doubleday, 1995)

Dix, Dom Gregory; *The Shape of the Liturgy* (Continuum, 1945)

Dorsett, Lyle W.; *E.M. Bounds: Man of Prayer* (Zondervan, 1991)

Encyclopaedia Britannica, 1911; Vol. 14 (Ireland, Church of; Page 789)

Englebert, Omer; *St. Francis of Assisi: A Biography*; Translated from the French by Eve Marie Cooper (Servant Books, 1979)

Hunter III, George G.; *The Celtic Way of Evangelism: How Christianity Can Reach the West...Again* (Abingdon Press, 2000)

International Standard Bible Encyclopedia, 1915; Orr, James, M.A., D.D., General Editor (Entry for: "Hours of Prayer" by Henry E. Dosker)

Lewis, C.S.; *Reflections On the Psalms* (HarperOne, 2017)

Michael, Larry J.; *Spurgeon On Leadership* (Kregel Academic & Professional, 2nd Edition, 2010)

Moorhouse, Geoffrey; *Sun Dancing: Life in a Medieval Monastery and How Celtic Spirituality Influenced the World* (Harcourt Brace & Company, 1997)

Oden, Thomas; General Editor; *Ancient Christian Doctrine,* Vol. 1-5 (IVP Academic, 2009)

Oden, Thomas, General Editor; *Ancient Christian Commentary On Scripture,* 29 Volumes (InterVarsity Press, 2005)

Papavassiliou, Vassilios; (Commentary on) Climacus, St. John; *Thirty Steps to Heaven: The Ladder of Divine Ascent for All Walks of Life* (Ancient Faith Publishing, 2014)

Pelikan, Jaroslav; *The Christian Tradition,* Vols. 1-5 (University of Chicago Press, 1971)

Pelikan, Jaroslav; *Credo* (Yale University Press, 2003)

Philokalia, The; Vols. 1-4 (Faber and Faber, 1983)

Preston, S.G.; *Prayer as a Total Lifestyle* (PrayerFoundation Press, 2018)

Preston, S.G.; *Prayer as a Celtic Lay Monk* (PrayerFoundation Press, 2018)

Schaff, Philip; *History of the Christian Church,* Vols. 1-8 (Hendrickson, 2006).

Steer, Roger; *George Müller: Delighted in God* (Christian Focus, Revised Edition, 2015)

S.G. Preston

Index:

(*Note:* there are no entries for certain words -- including *Christ*, *Holy Spirit*, *Christianity*, *Bible*, and *Prayer*; because they are mentioned or implied on nearly every page.)

A

S.G. Preston

C

D

E

F

Facebook (Internet); 53
Fairy-tales; 191
Faithfulness; 116, 142, 144, 146, 153, 170, 196, 209
Family Relationship; 59, 67, 68
Fasting; ii, 170, 174
Fern-seed and Elephants; (Essays) by C.S. Lewis; ii, 193
Felicity (Martyr); 108
Fever; 83
First Apology by Justin Martyr (Early Christian Worship); 159, 160, 161
Flavia Neapolis (Today's Nablus, Israel); 159
Florida; 22, 42, 50, 101, 155, 209
Flossenburg Prison (Bonhoeffer); 130
Footwashing by Christ (Forgiveness); 80
Footwear Removed Before Worship (Early Church); 162
Found (Daughter and Little Boy); 142
France; 72, 118, 130
Francis of Assisi, St.; 10, 32, 102, 104, 129
Franciscan Lutheran Community Chapel (Florida); 101
Friends of God; 55
Fruit of the Holy Spirit; 56, 128

G

Gaelic (Old Saying, Proverb, Prayer); 232
Gall Bladder Operation; 147
Gateway Films (Ken Curtis, Founder; Bill Curtis, President); 241
Genesis; 220, 221, 228, 229, 236
Gentiles; 221
George Muller: Delighted in God by Roger Steer; 236
Georgia (Country of); 123
German Lutheran (Dietrich Bonhoeffer); 175
Germany; 76, 129, 131, 158, 220
G.I. Bill; 140
Gibson, Mel (Film: *Passion of the Christ*); 118
Gladiator; 108
Gland Swollen; 109
Goiter, Multi-Nodular; 142
Goldendale, Washington; 147
Gomorrah; 229
Good News; 100, 172, 176
Gospel for Asia; 121
Gospel in China; 84
Gospel in Portland; 81

H

L

M

N

O

R

S

W

X

Y

Z

Pax Et Bonum!

May God richly bless you as you continue to serve Him!

Yours in Christ,

-Lay Monk Preston & Lay Monk Linda